E.A.G.

Notes on Portugal

E.A.G.

Notes on Portugal

ISBN/EAN: 9783337289591

Printed in Europe, USA, Canada, Australia, Japan

Cover: Foto ©Thomas Meinert / pixelio.de

More available books at **www.hansebooks.com**

NOTES on PORTUGAL.

BY E. A. G.

PHILADELPHIA :

PHILADELPHIA CATHOLIC PUBLISHING COMPANY,

1876.

UR purpose in making this publication, was to present a collection of considerations and statistical details, which might lead the reader to, at least, an approximate comprehension of the situation of Portugal in the concourse of civilized nations.

For that, we have had recourse to competent works, and have taken much from that of Sr. Teixeira de Vasconcellos, a distinguished writer, and of Sr. de Figueiredo, a very eminent consular functionary. In addition, the excellent report of the Commercial Association of Lisbon, for 1874, and some official documents have served as guides.

Our department of Statistics is not yet very prolific in information, and we are greatly in need of a work like the "Annuaire de la Belgique," in which could be found the surest and most exact details in all the branches of the administration. A step has been taken in that direction; but a long time will elapse before anything of importance is effected.

There are in Portugal very good books on the history of that country, and meritorious works in French are also to be found, such as those of Ferdinand Denis, Buchot, Voegel, etc. ; but in the English language, we believe our publication is the first of the kind, as we cannot affirm that the "Travels in Portugal," by Latouche, or the work of Lady Jackson are similar to this one.

The reader will find here some facts connected with the history of Portugal not known to many persons outside of that country. One of these is the discovery of Australia by the Portuguese. It is commonly supposed that La Pérouse was the first discoverer. Whether that was the case or not, we leave the intelligent reader to determine, when he has perused what is said concerning it in the Appendix.

NOTES ON PORTUGAL.

INTRODUCTION.

Despite the glorious part that has been played by the Portuguese in the history of Europe, and notwithstanding the magnificent colonial empire founded by them in South America, the inhabitants of North America know very little concerning the small kingdom of Portugal. Americans are somewhat apt to judge of a country by its extent alone. Possibly this mode of estimating the strength and importance of a nation may be natural to a race possessing the most magnificent domain, but it is not always just. In the case of Portugal, we err greatly if we consider that country to possess an importance proportionate only to its extent. If we except a certain category of distinguished personages, who have made themselves acquainted with European events, we shall find that even well-informed Americans are cognizant of merely its existence as a part of Europe, confined on the West and South by an immensely greater neighbor—Spain, with which they imagine it is in some way connected. They do not concede to it an independent existence, but confound its destinies in respect to political, economical and social life, with those of Spain.

Portugal has always desired to live in amity with its neighbor, a nation of the same race; but the student in history will find that the two kingdoms of the Iberian Peninsular have, up to the present, pursued two paths as distinct from each other, as are their customs, natures and aspirations.

There are in Portugal all the conditions befitting a truly independent nation. The Portuguese, firm in their love of country, and inspired by their traditions, could not even suppose that their right to exist in an independent state would be questioned. Portugal, in their eyes, is complete mistress of her destinies, and exercises fully her dominion. "We live, and we have always lived, having our political interests completely distinct from those of Spain."

The words we have just cited have never penetrated in their proper sense, the minds of those writers who, ill-informed, to say the least, affirm quite the contrary.

We have read, in a very influential paper published in New York, the following words contained in an article entitled "Spain":— "The destinies of the two nations have been identical in the same manner as their political interests and history." To reply triumphantly to such an assertion, it will suffice to repeat the remarkable words that Senor Estevan Collantes, the Ambassador from Spain at Lisbon, pronounced when presenting his credentials to the Portuguese monarch: "Portugal owes her happiness to her popular king as well as to her free institutions. Spain desires to follow in the same road."

Nay, more. In the reply given by Alphonsus XII., to the address of the Portuguese Ambassador who had come to congratulate him on his elevation to the throne, we find the following words: "Relying upon the great majority of the Spaniards, I am resolved to re-establish peace, and with it found the proper institutions of a constitutional monarchy, in order, that under their influence, *and in the same manner as they succeeded in your noble land,* there may be developed the germs of wealth which this country contains. In this way the commercial relations existing between Spain and Portugal will strengthen still more the bonds of friendship, which ought always to exist between two nations, independent, indeed, but brothers on account of a common origin."

The improvements in both morals and strength, to which all well-governed nations aspire, have been already undertaken by Portugal, and on a close examination it will be ascertained that these endeavors have not been fruitless.

The American people cannot but sympathize with a nation, which is indeed small as regards territory, but is illustrious on account of its glorious traditions and its constant struggle in the field of investigation and enterprise. Celebrated discoveries and conquests symbolized by the intimate union of the sword with, the Cross, cnobled the ancient Portuguese. *"In hoc signo vinces"* was the legend that led them when they sought new countries. Unlike the other nations of Europe they did not found simply factories in the lands they conquered, but animated by religious zeal, they planted in the new world the standard of the Cross, and taught to the ignorant tribes that morality of Christianity which is at once so sublime and so sweet.

The fleets of Portugal ploughed the stormy main, bearing her bold sailors to magnificent discoveries. Whilst producing Vasco de Gama, and Alphonsus d' Albuquerque, a poet worthy of the time, appeared in the person of Luiz de Camoens. The exploits of the Portuguese argonauts demanded a fitting minstrel. The Lusiades will be for ever the greatest monument of their glories, and the sublimest epic of the Peninsula.

After a long period of prosperity, the storms of misfortune fell upon the country and reduced it to the second rank. The Marquis de Pombal raised his native land from the depths of despair. But this elevation was for only a short time. The wars with Napoleon, the loss of Brazil and of other colonies, and civil contentions, all combined to reduce Portugal to misery and distraction.

Despite all these circumstances, there existed in the hearts of the people an earnest patriotism which kept alive the flame of nationality. The love of independence reigned supreme. Out of chaos came forth order, and to-day, Portugal stands before the world, ready to enter upon a grand career. Several things remain to be done ; certain shackles must be thrown off and various abuses eliminated. Already she has instituted a reform in her financial matters, thereby acquiring the esteem of the enlightened world. Nor has the question of educating her lower classes been neglected. In truth, in regard to that subject as well as to the solution of the problem concerning the union of religion with the civil authority, she shows an example that might be studied very profitably by those states of Europe which are afflicted with ecclesiastical and educational disputes.

Nor have the material improvements been neglected. Rail-roads are being constructed, the high roads improved, and lines of steamships established between the metropolis and the colon-ial possessions. Thus are enlarged the commercial transactions, the incentive of which depend upon facility of communication and cheapness of transportation. A great number of banks and other institutions of credit, convenient to agriculture as well as to the growing industries, has been founded.

With a large population, situated in the extreme west of Europe, and possessing one of the best seaports in the world ; having islands admirably situated in the road to the two Americas ; Sovereign of vast colonies in Western and Eastern Africa, India, China and Oceanica, Portugal can and ought to be considered as a State of the greatest importance among the powers of the second rank.

The relations between the United States and Europe are increasing at rapid strides. Attracted by its sympathy with the Democratic movement, summoned by its vast commercial interests to unite itself still more with the Old World, and impelled by its own greatness to enter into the grand development of civilization, and into the political life of the European States, the great Republic requires a secure and free access to Europe. Geograpically, Portugal occupies the same position to North America as Belgium does to Great Britain. Being in the most direct route, Portugal is that State of Europe with which the most profitable relations could be maintained.

The varied productions of Portugal should be adverted to. On the mountains we find the pine, the oak, the chestnut and all the flora natural to an elevated region ; everywhere else— cereals and fruits of all kinds, grapes, olives, oranges, figs, dates, grenadines, etc. A slight effort alone is necessary to naturalize the equinoctial plants. Formerly Portugal afforded nourishment to a great number of the Spaniards, and was called by Cæsar the Sicily of Spain. But owing to neglect, the natural resources of the country have not been turned to great utility during the past few centuries. If it is true that Geography throws light upon, and even dominates history, is there a single country to which this observation could be better applied than Portugal. Hemmed in between Spain and the ocean, removed from the general interests of European States, how could it aspire to play an important role upon the continent? But the immensity of the ocean displays itself before it and seems to encourage adventure. It is then upon its fleets that the future and the glory of the Lusitanian race depend.

The history of Portugal is explained by her Geographical position.

Description of Portugal.

Situated at the extremity of the Iberian Peninsular and consequently of the European Continent, Portugal extends from 8°.46′ to 11°.51′ in longitude, and from 36.58′ to 42.°7′ in latitude, thus covering a space of about 34,500 square miles. On the north and east the Spanish provinces of Galicia, Valladolid, Zamora, Salamanca, Estramadura and Seville, form a limit; on the west, the broad Atlantic presents a wide expanse of water, on which, let us hope, future fleets will be wafted to the Tagus, in as imposing armadas as they were wont to do.

Its most striking physical feature is displayed in its mountainous appearance. Indeed, in all parts of the country, mountains tower aloft. Unlike Spain, the plains are of small dimensions, The ranges rise in Spain and, for the most part, run parallel to the Pyrenees, terminating at the Atlantic. Its rivers likewise follow the same direction. The mountains, which are chiefly composed of the ranges of Montesinho, Estrella, Cintra, and Monchique, present incontestable proofs of their volcanic origin. They abound in quarries of marble, rivalling the Pentelican; in mines of gold, silver, iron, copper and lead, and above all, in hot and in mineral springs. Whilst speaking about the last mentioned subject, namely, springs, we should mention that, in St. Michael, one of the Azores, the celebrated waters called "das Furnas" are extremely beneficial for the diseases of the skin, rheumatism, scrofula, and others of the like description. On the summits of these mountains we find the two principal lakes, of which circumstances the poets have not failed to take advantage. Lago Grande has furnished an inexhaustible theme. The ranges, moreover, enclose a multitude of fertile valleys. These valleys are to be found principally in the province of Beira. Frequently these pleasant spots are devasted by terrible earthquakes. Portugal, alas! has reason to dread these dreadful phenomena of nature. We might mention those in 1356, 1597 and in 1755. The last one was the most calamitous. By it the City of Lisbon was destroyed, and the whole of Portugal thrown into mourning. The Azores and Madeira, also, afford examples of volcanic action. The island of Pico, one of the western Azores, is dominated by a volcano, which elevates itself to a height of 7,500 feet.

Three of its most important rivers take their rise in Spain, viz.: the Tagus, the Douro and the Guadiana. These empty themselves into the Atlantic, as do all the other streams. We have also the Lima—so famous formerly under the name of Lethe—the Mondego, the Ave, the Sado, the Tamega, the Agueda, the Erjes, and the Bezere. The majority of these streams are merely torrents, alternately surcharged by the melted snows of the mountains, and dried up by the heat of the sun.

We now come to the various Provinces. They are as follows: Minho, or Minho e *Douro*, Tras-os-Montes, Beira, Estremadura, Alemtejo, and Algarves. The last province gives the title of king, which the monarchs of Portugal bear in addition to their more usual one.

The Climate of Portugal is variable according to the districts. But it is, upon the whole, one of the finest in Europe. We do not meet with the oppressive heats that reign in countries situated in the same latitude. It is only the interior which suffers somewhat from the heat of the sun and from drouth. This, however, is owing to the want of the forests. Cold is not felt anywhere, except in the highest districts of the north. Snow and ice are looked upon as curiosities, and the rivers are never frozen over.

The seasons present a few peculiarities. There are what we might call two springs during the year. The first commences in February. During the next three months, a dry heat alternates with stormy weather; in general, however, soft and continued rains are not common. The harvest takes place in June, except in the mountainous districts of the north-east, where that time is July. This is also the period of the greatest heat, varying from a minimum of 20° Centigrade to a maximum of 40° Centigrade. Then the want of rain and the heat of the sun dry up the vegetation. But at the end of September the equinoctial rains commence, being followed in October by the second summer. Then burst forth the leaves, and flowers bedeck the orange trees. The heaviest rains fall in November and December. The coldest month of the year is January. Another peculiarity is that thunder-storms do not occur in the summer, but during the winter.

The climate of the Azores and Madeira, although warmer on account of the latitude, is neither less agreeable nor less salubrious than that of the Portuguese Continent; the remarkable serenity of the sky attracts thither from the north of Europe many invalids suffering from consumption. It must be admitted, however that there have been a few epidemics. In 1857 the yellow fever, brought from Brazil, caused dreadful ravages. But these scourges would not have occurred, had there not been a preparation made for them in the shape of defective sanitary arrangements. Improve the drainage and sewerage, and typhus, with its concomitant evils, will become unknown.

The Azores and Madeira form two provinces adjacent to the
Portuguese mainland, governed in exactly the same manner as
the rest of the kingdom. They do not possess, in the slightest
degree, the character of colonies. The island of Madeira, known
to this country through its wines especially, is 18 league long
and 8 wide. The surface is mountainous, but of a tropical fertility; as to the climate, it is so temperate and uniform, that
consumptives find there the means of prolonging their existence
and even of being cured, in the instances where the disease has
not advanced too far. Sugar cane and vine constitute the principal productions. The exportation of wines, before the *oidium
tunkeris,* was annually about 12,000 pipes. The most renowned
qualities are Malvasia, Serceal and Tinto. After having endured
the vine-disease for several years, many proprietors commenced
to plant sugar-cane, the cultivation of which had been abandoned
almost entirely. Cereals do not succeed in Madeira, and there is
consequently, a large amount imported. On the other hand, the
fruits and plants of Europe, Asia and Africa are well developed
in that island, thanks to favorable climatic influences. The
city of Funchal, the principal place on the island, is much re-
sorted to by foreigners, especially the English, the population is
distinguished for its refined manners.

Gonçalo Velho Cabral, in 1432, discovered the isle of St.
Maria, which discovery led to that of the Archipelago of the
Azores. The latter event took place 1449, or in 1460, according to the various opinions. The name Azores was given
because of the number of goshawks, which were seen floating in
the air: the arms of the Archipelago consist of a goshawk sur-
rounded by nine stars, representing the niue constituent islands.
They were peopled by Portuguese and Flemings, and were formed
into fiefs held by noblemen, who acknowledged only the king.
They are 200 leagues distant from Portugal, 38°, 38′ latitude
and 29° 32′ longtitude, and are for the most part, volcanic.

The soil is generally very fertile, as are all soils which proceed
from the decomposition of basalt, and whose formation comes
from volcanoes. Although very mountainous, we find it rich
in exceedingly fertile valleys. The climate less dry than that
of Madeira, is, however, very healthy, and causes longevity
Indian corn, wheat, potatoes, yams, oranges, and wines, constitute the chief agricultural wealth. Tobacco also is grown with
success. Cochineal and the culture of silk worms would be
very important sources of wealth, if serious attention were paid
to them. The best known ports are Horta, Angra, and Ponta
Delgada. The bay of Horta is the best for navigation. A
dock is about to be constructed for that place, which will
render immense service to the navigation of the world. Several
unfortunate circumstances prevented these islands from being
more developed. They were in past times often attacked by the
barbaric corsairs, and they had to undergo, on several occasions,
cruel ravages caused by volcanic eruptions. Frequently by
reason of these eruptions islets were formed, which however
soon disappeared beneath the waves, despite the standard of
Her Britannic Majesty which the English have the habit of
planting on all *treasure trove.*

Formerly Terceira was the Capital of the whole Archipelago
and it is yet the seat of a Bishopric and of a military division.
It was in this island that the liberal troops commenced their
exploits against the armies of D. Miguel. The island is called,
like Oporto, the bulwark of Portuguese liberty. Indeed it must
be said that the Archipelago has always shown itself full of
patriotic sentiments. In taking the part of D. Antonio, Prior
of Crato who was the natural candidate against the usurpation
of Philip II of Spain, and in pronouncing, later on, so ener-
getically for the restoration of the Braganzas in 1640, the
inhabitants of the Azores have often deserved well of the father-

land. The city of Augra has borne the title of "Sempre leal" since the reign of John IV.

Terceira has lost much of its ancient importance. Its port has never been so famous as that of Horta. S. Michael has became by its wealth, the first in the groups of the Azores; it is the largest as well as the most densely populated.

The island which has the most intercourse with the United States, is that of Fayal. The name of an illustrious American citizen, the late Consul, Charles S. Dabney, will always remain venerated by the country of his adoption.

To finish this glance at the Azores, we might say that the home administrations have sometimes neglected to give satisfaction to all their needs. But it should not be imagined, on that account, that the Fayalese are the less attached to their fatherland. Patriotism burns with as intense a flame within the breasts of the Fayalese as in the hearts of the inhabitants of the metropolis.

ʜISTORICAL ꜱKETCH.

The father-land of the ancient Lusitanians, brothers of the Celtiberians and cousins of the other Celtic races, through the common bonds which the Gaelic root established between all the nations of that great family, Portugal had attracted, at various epochs, the Phoenicians and the Carthaginians, before mighty Rome succeeded in subduing the greater portion of the Iberian Peninsula. It was only after severe struggles that the Lusitanians were finally overcome by the Romans. But they fell gloriously. The name of Viriathus is one of the noblest in their history. From the time he escaped from the base massacre of thirty thousand Lusitanians by Servilius Galba, till his assassination (140 B. C.), the Romans encountered one whose name spread fear amongst their legions. When the hero fell, murdered by two of his own soldiers, the contest was not quite ended. Even the women fought with desperate courage. We must pass rapidly over the history of Portugal under the Romans. From the moment Spain became Roman, Lusitania ceased to have a history of its own; it was merely one of the finest provinces of the Empire. On account of its situation, it was free from both the civil contentions which soon desolated the Roman Universe, and the inroads of the barbarians; its prosperity was almost constant. Magnificent monuments attest this happy state. Look at the aqueduct at Evora, the temple of Diana, the baths at

Cintra and the Amphitheatre of Lisbon. However, the Empire began to fall into pieces. Gaul first felt the evils of the formidable attacks of the rude northern tribes; the turn of Spain followed and the Vandals, Suevi and Vieigoths were delayed but a short time at the Pyrenees. These were succeeded in 711 by the Arabs, who retained a firm hold until the commencement of the 11th century. The Christian princes then began to recover from the Paynim, by force of arms, the territory lying between the Minho and the Douro. In 1095 Alphonsus VI, king of Leon and of Castille, after having married his daughter to a prince of the house of Hugh Capet, Henry of Burgundy, who had come to seek fortune in the Peninsula by fighting the Moors, created the chivalric foreigner count of this same district increased by a portion of the province of Beira, and which from that time bore the name of Portugal. At the death of his father-in-law and sovereign, Henry made his power independent and hereditary. He achieved rapid conquests and his son Alphonsus I, still more fortunate, completely defeated the Moors, near Ourique in 1139: but more important advantages, gained over his cousin and sovereign Alphonsus VII, king of Leon and Castille, whom the Cortes of Leon had proclaimed emperor, acquired for him the title of king. Alphonsus I, being frequently engaged in war with the former sovereigns of the country, declared himself vassal of the Holy See, in order to strengthen himself against their demands. His campaigns against the Moors were crowned with success by the capture of Santarem and of Lisbon in 1147. He died in 1185. The kingdom was extended by his successors, until it contained nearly its present area.

We find that the direct line came to an end in 1383, when the crown fell into the hands of John I, natural son of Peter I, who was proclaimed king by the cortes. John I. strengthened his throne by the brilliant victory of Aljubarrota gained over the

Castilians. Then commenced the maritime and colonial power
of Portugal. By his queen, Philippa of Lancaster, he had
several sons. The eldest, Edward, succeeded him in 1433; but
the most celebrated was Henry the Navigator, who, during the
consecutive reigns of his brother and of his nephew Alphonsus
V, was the promoter of all the maritime expeditions, and thus
pushed on the greatness of the nation.

The first exploits were the taking of Ceuta in Morocco, in
1415; the discovery of Madeira and Porto Santo in 1419. Of
the Azores in 1432, and of the Cape Verd in 1460. It was
during the reign of John II, the Perfect, that the Portuguese
monarchy entered into full enjoyment of power. The discovery
of the Cape of Good Hope in 1486, by Bartholomeu Diaz, marked
a new era. The negro sovereigns on the coasts of Africa had
submitted to John II. It was on the ocean, the true theatre of
Portuguese glory, that John II concentrated almost exclusively
his ambitious projects. Having assumed the title of "Lord of Guinea," he had various expeditions led against the Moors in Africa.
The brilliant success of the Portuguese generals was eclipsed only
by the marvellous progress which the Portuguese marine had made
on the other side of the equator. It had been remarked by the
navigators, when they arrived in the neighborhood of that famous
line, that Africa went on increasing towards the west, and the
eager desire to ascertain the truth soon removed all ideas of
doubt. From Guinea the Portuguese were not long in advancing
to the kingdom of Benin, and thence to the Congo. At length,
on the second of August, 1486, Bartholomeu Diaz set sail with
two ships and a tender. Tormented by the vague reports that
had come to him concerning a king named Prester John, the
King of Portugal had charged that distinguished navigator to
go and verify the legends of which this mysterious personage
was the object. Bartholomeu scrupulously followed the instructions he had received, but was unable to ascertain any pertinent

information from the inhabitants along the coast. However, he continued on his course, despite the most terrible tempests and the protests of even the hardy mariners that accompanied him. The result of his constancy was glorious. After various delays and annoyances he finally reached a cape which he called the Cape of Torments. Even then, he was not satisfied and the voyage would have been extended, had he not encountered the determined refusal of his companions.

After an absence of seventeen months, he returned home. John II, delighted with his recital and prescient of future benefits to be derived from the discovery, hastened to change the mournful name "Cape of Torments" into that of "Cape of Good Hope."

Whilst this great enterprise was being pursued, a no less important discovery, or to speak more properly, series of discoveries, was being prosecuted in the East. Diaz endeavored to unravel the mystery of Prester John by sea, but two other Portuguese, Pedro de Covilham and Alphonsus de Paiva, attempted to solve the same question, by land. At Cairo they separated—Alphonsus for Ethiopia; Covilham for the Indies. The former was unfortunate in his efforts and soon died. His comrade touched at Cananor, Calicut and Goa, was the first to learn what the Indies actually were, traversed the vast ocean which separates them from Africa, visited Sofala, and returned to Aden with the most precious news.

Having arrived at length in Cairo, he prepared to embark for Portugal, full of sorrow for the death of Paiva, when a Spanish Jew came to him on the part of John II., and treated of Babylon, Bagdad, and Ormuz. Covilham yielded, and having committed his papers to the Jew, he set out anew. Having traveled for some time, he disappeared in Abyssinia.

These voyages of Covilham deserve a distinguished rank among the great works of that epoch. Although he did not succeed in verifying the fables about Prester John, he had the honor of being the first Christian to traverse the oceans of the East. It could no longer be doubted that Africa was circum-navigable, and that it was possible to open a new road to the Indies.

But we must retrace our steps and treat of that greatest dis-covery of modern times—the discovery of America. On a certain day in 1493, John II., was startled by the news of the arrival in the port of Lisbon, of two vessels bearing the arms of Castille, and driven by tempests to seek shelter. They were those of Christopher Columbus, who carried with him the most striking proofs of his wonderous success. Great grief filled the breast of John, when he remembered that he entertained preju-dices against Columbus, when that great man offered to execute for Portugal what he had just accomplished for Castille; thus losing possession of a whole world, which the Castilians had acquired by a single stroke, whereas, the Portuguese had pursued the same end for 80 years. But despite his chagrin, he had a generous heart. He refused the unworthy suggestions of his evil counsellors, who wished him to hide in the blood of Colum-bus the marvellous secret. He received the distinguished navi-gator at his court, bestowed honors on him, and finally dismissed him to his own sovereign, with ample tokens of his regard.

Although the Portuguse lost the honor of discovering America, to them belongs the merit of having prepared the way. The initiative to that enterprise, as well to the doubling of the Cape of Good Hope, had been given by the establishment of the cele-brated school at Sagres, founded by the Infante Don Henrique.

Christopher Columbus had had his imagination inflamed by the wonderful narrative of the explorations and conquests of the Portuguese. Before he undertook the famous voyage, the result of which was to add a new world to the old, he had married in Lisbon, in 1471, the daughter of the celebrated navigator Perestrello, whose charts and memoirs undoubtedly contributed to the realization of the plan conceived and carried out by the bold and indefatigable adventurer. It will be seen that in less than half a century, Portugal had conquered 4,500 leagues of coast, captured Ormuz at the entrance of the Persian Gulf, and Socotra at the mouth of the Red Sea, thus closing against the Mussulmans and Venice, the ancient roads to Hindoostan and Indo-China, and diverting to its own advantage a commerce which had been established for more than twenty centuries. Alphonsus de Albuquerque went so far as to conceive the project of diverting the course of the Nile into the Red Sea in order to prevent commerce from following its ancient direction.

The discoveries and the geographical labors of the Portuguese opened to the other nations of Europe the highway of the seas. It was the dawn of the renaissance. We had already entered into modern history in which Portugal has since played no unimportant part. Although deprived of the honor of discovering America, the subjects of John II., inspired by their monarch's enthusiasm, did not hesitate to take advantage of the new opening for enterprise.

John ordered a fleet to be immediately equipped, in order that it might follow over the traces of the Spaniards. He hoped, by reason of the incontestable superiority of his marine, that the fruits of the success of Columbus would return to himself, and that the ocean would not cease to be Portuguese. But Castille hastened to exclaim against this supposed usurpation of its rights, and it was found necessary for the Pope to act as mediator. The treaty of Tordesillas divided the world into two hemispheres, one of which (the Eastern) was to belong to Portugal, and the other (the Western) to Spain.

John, assured of the possession of the East, determined to regain his former superiority by making vast conquests in Asia. He therefore had an important squadron prepared, and gave its command to his most skillful mariner, Vasco da Gama.   But he did not live to see the fruits of his enterprise.

Our space does not allow us to make more than a passing eulogium on this great monarch.   Although surnamed Perfect, he had the greater part of the faults of the time, and pushed justice to even rigor.   But he practised with a constant zeal and great success, his trade as king in the XVth century.   To lower the nobility, to unite himself to the people, and to maintain peace with the rest of the Peninsula, in order to consecrate to the ocean all the resources of his states, constituted the wisest policy of the king of Portugal.   It was he who prepared the splendors of the Portuguese Monarchy.   He possessed that attribute common to all great men, an ardent love of letters and art, so that it was his constant aim to attract to his court, men distinguished in literature and the arts, of which, at that time, Italy alone possessed the precious store.   By him was the hitherto unknown taste for these embellishments introduced into the kingdom.

Several years elapsed before Vasco da Gama received from the succeeding king, Emmanuel the Fortunate, the signal of departure.   Vasco received the letters and instructions (among which were the memoirs and map of Covilhan) at Lisbon, and having taken Communion with his 160 companions, set forth towards his fleet.   It was on the 7th of July, 1497, that the four ships of Gama weighed anchor before the eyes of an immense multitude of people praying for their success.

At the time Vasco da Gama was directing his course toward the Indies, his enterprise was no less necessary than glorious. The commercial relations of Asia with the West, formerly so active and so prosperous at the period of Alexandria, Constantinople and Caffa had been nearly ruined, during the time those cities languished under the Mahommetan rule.   What little did exist, profited only Genoa, Florence, and, above all, Venice.

It was therefore indispensable that Europe herself should go, and without the mediation of the Italian republics or of the Turks, demand from the East those productions that were indispensable. In opening a new way to the commerce of Asia, and in destroying the monopoly of the Italian cities, the Portuguese navigators did not contribute to the glory and prosperity of only their land, they deserved the thanks of the whole West.

A northerly wind favored the little squadron, and it passed without trouble the Canaries, the Cape Verd islands, touched at St. Helena, where it remained a short time, and finally reached the Cape of Good Hope. When arrived there the daring navigators were agreeably surprised to find that instead of dreadful tempests, they experienced delightful weather. This circumstance inspired them with new confidence, and they advanced with ardor over the hitherto unknown seas. Having touched along the African coast at various parts, amongst which were the coasts of Natal, Mozambique and Melinda, Gama set sail for the shores of India, where he arrived on the 20th of May, 1498. The spot at which he landed, is a few miles to the north of Calicut on the Malabar coast. His reception by the Zamorin of Calicut was not, on the whole, very satisfactory, owing to the cabals of the Arabian merchants, who were jealous of what they felt to be the overpowering ascendancy of the Portuguese. But some enterchange of goods, etc., furnished sufficient grounds for believing that the discovery would greatly redound to the power and the glory of Portugal. The hardy adventurers soon found it necessary to abandon the country for the present, and to return to Europe for the necessary reinforcements.

The homeward voyage was devoid of remarkable incidents. It might be mentioned, however, that owing to a mistake in regard to relative positions caused by a frightful tempest, Vasco de Gama lost the opportunity of being the first to tell the news. Coelho, captain of the "Berrio," arrived first in Lisbon, on the

29th of July, 1499. Vasco arrived a month later. His return was a triumph. Emmanuel covered him with honors, and Vasco de Gama become Don Vasco, Count de Vidigueira and Grand Admiral of all the Indian Seas.

No time was lost, and the command of the squadron sent to gather the fruits of the glorious discovery, was given to Pedro Alvarez Cabral. On the 8th of March, 1500, the expedition, consisting of 12 ships, set sail. Cabral followed the course indicated by his illustrious predecessor ; but a sudden tempest carrying him to the westward, threw him upon an unknown coast. He called the spot Porto Seguro, and the country Santa Cruz. Being satisfied with merely admiring the beauty of the country, he thought he would succeed in accomplishing, by chance, the project entertained for so long a time by Christopher Columbus, viz.: of going to India by the western route. The land he had touched at and treated with so much indifference, is known to-day as Brazil, in South America, never before seen by a European. Thus chance assisted genius in revealing to man all the mysteries of the globe.

Although important events occurred during the remainder of the voyage, the discovery of the South American continent was by far the most fortunate result. The Zamorin of Calicut continuing hostile, the Portuguese, after severe losses, determined to seek an asylum with the king of Cochin China. The latter being engaged in war with his lord paramount, was glad to re-receive such allies. An alliance was formed with the king of Cananor. In this manner, by fomenting rivalry between the various States of India, the Europeans succeeded in obtaining possession of those vast regions. The French, English, and Dutch were only the imitators of the Portuguese, when they pursued this policy.

Having thus established relations with a few of the princes, Cabral at length weighed anchor, and after a long series of frightful tempests, arrived in the Tagus with the debris of his squadron.

Sufficient was now learned to make it appearant to Emmanuel that although there were great difficulties to surmount, there was also a grand empire to be founded by him in India. Uniting promptness with energy, and being determined to venture for success under the most favorable auspices, he summoned Vasco de Gama himself to the command of a magnificent armada consisting of 20 well armed ships. The expedition was successful in all respects. The first thing was to spread the terror of the Portuguese name at Sofala, Mozambique, Melinde, and wheresoever treachery had been displayed. The report of his severity had preceded him to Cananor, so that his reception there was friendly in the extreme. Thence he hastened to Calicut, and having made the demand that all the Mussulmans should quit the kingdom, (which demand was not complied with) he opened fire on the devoted place. The city was half ruined before the Zamorin felt constrained to sue for a cessation of hostilities. The Portuguese then made sail for Cochin China. There, all were friendly, and the alliance was confirmed. But it must be confessed that his cruelty effected the treaty. The superiority his conduct assured him throughout Malabar, was still further strengthened by a great naval victory which he gained over an immense force sent against him by the Zamorin of Calicut.

When Gama, for the second time, quitted Hindoostan, he was able to congratulate himself on having planted the seeds of a mighty empire.

We cannot follow the Portuguese in their career of victory. We should, however, mention the names of some of the great captains of whom Portugal was so prolific at that time. The names of Eduardo Pacheco, Alphonsus d' Albuquerque, the conqueror of India and the hero of Camoens, d' Almeida, and Menezes, shine in the first rank of the nobility as well as on the

pages of the history of Portugal. Titles of nobility continued to
be one of the recompenses reserved for great services to the State.
Vasco de Gama, become Don Vasco and Count, was a striking
proof of this, and his name reflects additional honor upon Emmanuel, a king, who despite his defects, knew how to make use .
of men of genius.

Few nations can present such a spectacle as Portugal offered
at the time of the death of Emmanuel the Fortunate. What
a marvellous picture! Out of the midst of a small nation,
until then but little known to the world, suddenly sprung
intrepid navigators and great generals. As a reward for their
boldness, we see Africa mapped out, the East Indies attached to
Europe, the southern portion of America discovered, Oceanica
subdued, the routes to India changed, or to speak more properly,
supplemented, the monoply of the Italian Republics ruined,
and Lisbon made the capital of commerce; whilst Christianity
spreading out beyond its former limits, advanced to the regeneration of the whole world. It seems to be a fable. Never have
such magnificent successes been gained with such feeble means
in so short a space of time, never has the strength of genius and
of courage been more gloriously exemplified. Indeed, the history of Portugal required not a historian, but a poet, for it reads
more like an epic than a narrative. The deeds of glory found
a fitting minstrel in the person of Camoens. He did not invent,
he related. The reality was beyond the powers of fiction. The
history of Portugal, at this period, is the history of heroism.

In the midst of these splendors there were symptoms of a
decline. The emigration to the various conquered countries de-
peopled Portugal, and under John III, successor to Emmanuel,
industry suffered from want of men. Into the colonies, abuses
were gradually introduced, bad governors frequently appointed,
and the heroic fortitude of the Portuguese changed into a vul-
gar love of money and its concomitant evil, luxury. These

causes soon led to the decadence of their power in the East
Indies, although it was for a time raised up by Jão de Castro.
In Africa, Alcazar, Arzila, Saff, and Azamor were abandoned,
(1549), and only the strong cities of Ceuta, Tangiers, and Te-
tuan retained. These steps was taken principally because of the
contempt in which their African possessions were held, now that
India offered such a vast field. Even Brazil appeared to be of
little importance. Malefactors and abandoned women were the
chief elements of the European population when John III.
undertook to colonize it in order to counterbalance somewhat
the Spanish influence in America. It was only in 1549, however, that the number of European inhabitants was large
enough to be honored with a governor. Thomas de Souza,
with whom some Jesuits were appointed, was selected as governor. But the policy universally adopted of planting the
seeds of colonial empire in the shape of the refuse of society,
had excited in the numerous tribes, a common hatred of the
Portuguese name, as they deemed all the whites to be of the
same stamp. What an unwise policy! To think of colonizing
vanquished countries with such materials as are usually sent!
To endeavor to found a new society with what corrupts and de-
stroys the best established communities.

In vain did the soldiers of Souza contend against the preju-
dices of the Indians. The religious element alone succeeded in
bringing about a successful issue. The Jesuits, those indefatigable pioneers of religion, and consequently of civilization,
plunged fearlessly into the forests, announced to the angry
savages the good news of the Saviour, weaned them little by
little from idolatry, and by the example of their own virtues
showed them that all Europeans were not alike. In this conduct consists the principal glory of the Society of Jesus. At
length the armies of the governor, but above all, the preaching of the Gospel by the Missionaries, established on a solid

base the Portuguse rule in Brazil. For a long time, however, that land remained in the second rank of colonies, being
imperfectly known. The mines, rich in the precious metals and
in other minerals, remained undiscovered for a long period.

During the reign of Don Sebastian, at a time when Portugal
retained with difficulty the precious relics of her colonial empire, a project was entertained of renewing, on the coast of
Africa, the great expeditions of John I., and of Alphonsus V.
In vain did the wise men of the kingdom protest against this
imprudence. A small force departed in 1574, disembarked near
Tangiers, and gained several minor successes. But it was in
1578, that the grand effort was made. The decisive battle was
fought in the middle of the vast plain of Alcazar, on the 4th of
August, 1578. Despite the heroic courage of Sebastian, his imprudence, together with treachery on the part of some followers,
caused the ruin of the Portuguese. At first, success was on the
side of the Christians, and they penetrated in the first shock of
battle to the tent of Muley Moluc. But the end was a disastrous defeat. How many were killed, or how many were captured cannot be ascertained with any degree of certainty from
the contradictory statements of the contemporaneous writers.
But the material losses of the day are of secondary importance,
when we look at the results of the battle.

The news of the defeat spread consternation throughout the
land. All perceived that it was the ruin of not merely Don
Sebastian's army, but of Portugal. Farewell to glory. A fight
for national existence was about to commence. The empire so
miraculously acquired was destroyed, and complete destruction
threatened the national liberties, on account of the grasping ambition of mighty Spain. Camoens expressed the depth of uni-
versal grief, when, at the point of death, he exclaimed, "At least
I die with my country." It is a striking coincidence, that at

the very time Portugal lost her power, she lost also the most illustrous representative of her literature.

Then followed a period of anarchy and servitude. Phillip II. of Spain, perceiving the weak condition of his unhappy neighbor, determined to add their country to his already vast dominions. He commenced by caresses and gold ; but he took care to assist those devices by sending 22,000 men under the famous Don Fernando de Toledo, Duke of Alba. How could the Portuguese, divided and weakened by the loss of noble blood, squandered in the last expedition to Africa, oppose such immense power? But there were some Portuguese left, who were worthy of their ancestors. These noble men, under the leadership of Don Antonio, offered an obstinate defence. The end, however, was inevitable. In 1583, Portugal and all her colonies were compelled to acknowledge the power of Spain. Phillip was master of a considerable part of Europe, of all that had been discovered in America and in the Phillipines, and now we see him adding to these immense possessions, Portugal, the empire of the Indies, the Moluccas, with a crowd of commercial establishments from the Red Sea to Japan.

From 1585 to 1640, Portugal was a province of Spain and shared in the successes and disasters of that country. It was a ruinous period. To complete the destruction of the Portuguese power, it required only the loss of her ships and sailors. This final blow fell. Phillip II. of Spain, carried away by his eager desire to fulfil his intention of extending his dominion until the sun should never set on the Spanish possessions, determined to overwhelm England. An armada was prepared, to the completion of which, the unfortunate Portuguese were required to contribute all their naval strength. The result of this expedition is too well known to require a repetition of its history. Shattered by storms, and attacked incessantly by their weaker but more active foes, the Spaniards, and with them the Portuguese, beheld

the shores of Western Europe strewn with the wrecks of their
once gallant ships.

Thus by becoming Spanish, Portugal lost her supremacy at
sea, which supremacy passed to the English. Having lost her
finest ships, and her most skilful sailors, she had to endure the
sight of her coasts blockaded and her commerce intercepted. It
was in 1589 that the English, under Drake, appeared on the
coast for the first time. Although they brought Don Antonio
who, as has been mentioned, had defended his country to the
last, it must be confessed that the liberty of Portugal was subordinate to their desire for pillage, and to the fear, lest Portugal
should regain her freedom. Her immense colonies and numerous ships were objects of prey ; besides, commercial and maritime interests, rather than generosity, have always had the greatest
influence in the resolutions of the English. Having rid themselves of Don Antonio, whom they had in vain presented to the
oppressed Portuguese as liberator, the English did not trouble
themselves any farther about concealing their true intentions,
but commenced business on their own responsibility. In order
to assist the unfortunate people then languishing under the rule
of Spain, they pillaged Pernambuco, attacked the Azores, captured the fort of Arquin, on the coast of Africa, and confiscated
as Spanish all the Portuguese ships they encountered at sea, not
hesitating to vary these friendly acts by devastating several
times the unhappy country of which they declared themselves to
be the allies. Faro and all the south of Algarves, with Buarcos,
were visited with the usual results, by these allies, thus proving
to Portugal that she had no less to fear from her protectors than
from the tyranny of the Spanish Sovereign.

The Dutch and the English gathered the spoils of the colonial
Empire. The former made themselves masters of the East, and
acquired a part of Ceylon and Japan, in Asia ; Saint George de
la Mine, on the Gold coast, in Africa, and the half of Brazil, in

South America. Thus the sovereignty of the seas fell into the hands of the Dutch ; only to be passed on to the English, from whose hands it has at length passed and awaits the moment when the Great Republic of the West will turn her attention from petty party strife to a nobler prize than can be offered by demagogues, the lasting dominion of the Ocean.

Spain continued her exacting demands for money to such an extent that the people were reduced to extreme poverty, in many cases possessing no other food than that of bread and fruit. Despite the general weakness in regard to courage, and in forgetfulness of disproportionate forces, an insurrection burst forth during the period of servitude, which might have succeeded, had not John Duke of Bragauza, who was looked on as the heir to the throne, refused to join with the insurgents. It was in the city of Evora, in Alem–Téjo, that this insurrection took place. The Spanish garrison was driven out. But the city soon afterwards expiated cruelly this glorious initiative. The powerful Richelieu constantly incited the Portuguese to rise en masse, and promised to send fifty ships and eleven thousand men, if they would undertake to raise to the throne a prince of the blood royal. Pinto Ribeiro, the secretary to Don Juan, Duke of Braganza, endeavored to keep alive the flame of freedom, and succeeded in enrolling, as conspirators, Don Miguel d' Almeida, Don Antonio de Saldanha, Don Luis da Cunha, the Arch-Bishops of Lisbon, Don Antonio d' Almada, Don George de Mello, and his brother the Grand Huntsman, Don Rodriquez de Sâ, and many others of note. The conspiracy was carried on most secretly, so that no clear idea of the state of affairs reached the ears of the Spanish Minister, Olivares. On the morning of the 1st of December, 1640, the revolution broke out. Confined at first to Lisbon, it spread rapidly throughout the provinces which were not governed with much regard for the feelings of the population, and which consequently hated still more the Castilian name.

Everywhere sorrow and despair were replaced by joy and hope ; the period of slavery was over ; Portugal was born again.

The Duke of Braganza assumed the reins of sovereignty under the title of John IV., and was soon recognized by, and taken under the protection of, the Great Powers of Europe. Although independent again, Portugal had much to fear from the power of her neighbor, weakened though Spain had been by the gigantic follies of Phillip II. and of Olivares. But fortune continued to smile, and on the 26th of May, 1644, the work of Pinto Ribeiro was completed by the victory of Montijo, gained by the Portuguese under Mathias d' Albuquerque.

The independence of Portugal was here assured and it had been recognized by France, England, Holland and Sweden. But despite the powerful protection of France, she did not regain her colonies. Although Holland had political sympathies with Portugal in regard to European affairs, she did not hesitate to continue in her course of conquering the possessions of the Portuguese in Asia and in America. The original masters of Asia held only Diu, Calicut, Cochin, Cananor, Goa, Coulan, Chaul, Daboul and Macao. In Africa only Mozambique, Sofala, Melinda (which the Arabs soon after seized), the Congo, Angola, Benguela, Saint Paul de hoanda and the islands of Fernando Po, Gorea, Annobom. St. Thomas and Prince remained. But the richest jewel of the crown, Brazil, was saved chiefly through the efforts of Vieira, who defeated the Dutch so completely that they were glad to capitulate and agree to leave Brazil immediately, thus abandoning their great collection of military material at Pernambuco. This circumstance shed a kind of light on this reign.

The succeeding king, Don Alphons VI was of a feeble nature, and unable to govern his kingdom with any prospect of success. His mother, the celebrated Dona Luiza Gusman, acted as regent, and met with great success in the role she assumed.

France, occupied by other interests, was unable to extend to Portugal the favor and protection she had hitherto shown. Recourse was had to England ; a commercial and maritime nation and the natural ally of the enemies of Spain. A bargain was soon struck, by which the tutelage of Portugal was made complete. It was agreed between Dona Luiza and Charles II of England, that a force of about 1300 should be levied in the British Isles, on condition that the arms and necessary equipments should be bought in Great Britain. Thanks to this permission, the Court of Lisbon flattered itself that liberty was secured. It was not known at first what was the price of England's apparent generosity. The growing vasalage of Portugal became more nanifest in the following year. Under the pretext of uniting the houses of Stuart and Braganza, and of assisting the doomed country, Charles II. demanded 2,000,000 cruzados, and the valuable possessions of Tangiers in Africa, and of Bombay in India.

Dona Luiza did not retain the reins of power very long.

A conspiracy headed by Castelmelho, overthrew and compelled her to retire to a secluded life. Alphonsus,although assisting in her downfall, was not seated on his throne long. His brother, Don Pedro, compelled him to sign his abdication. That prince, after having borne the title of Regent for a short period, mounted the throne.

Now that some kind of peace was patched up with Spain, Portugal turned her eyes to the East, in the hope that the ancient splendor of Lisbon might return. But it was in vain. The rivals in Asia—France, England and Holland, were too powerful for Portugal to dream of profiting by their dissentions.

It was the same in the West, whence a ray of sunshine fell upon the Portuguese. The discovery of rich mines promised to more than compensate them for their losses in the East. Such would have been the case had hard work been thought of as well as gold and silver. Despite the example of Spain, ruined by her inordinate thirst for gold, the Portuguese, throwing on one side agriculture and industry, thought only of their mines. It was a fatal error. The treaty of Methuen, signed December 27th, 1703, contributed not a little to the impoverishment of the country. For by it the English obtained the right to export to Portugal all things requisite for it, receiving in return the wines of Portugal. But instead of assisting the Portuguese it completed their subordination, as they were unable, as well as too indolent, to compete with the manufactures of England. In time the mines of Brazil failed to produce sufficient to pay for the imports. England, on the other hand, did not consume a large quantity of the wines, so that the balance of trade was entirely in her favor. Whilst England thus levied a tax on Portuguese indolence, John V. added to the general distress by devoting the vast treasures chance had bestowed on him, to the construction of useless buildings and works. Although at first successful in war, he finally had reason to deplore having undertaken it.

The picture again is changed. A stop is made in the course to ruin. The successor of John, Joseph I, was of mediocre nature. He seemed little able to raise his country; and yet his reign figures among the most glorious periods of the Portuguese history. Why? On account of his having a great minister, and because, in default of some more eminent quality, he had the rare merit of never having withdrawn his fav orfrom him

This minister was Sebastian Joseph de Carvalho e Melho, afterwards Marquis de Pombal. Carvalho was born in Lisbon, May 13th, 1699, and belonged to a good family. After the usual course of study, etc., he was, to the astonishment of all, appointed Secretary to the London Embassy, in which position he acquitted himself so well, that he soon received the Embassy to Vienna. Whilst there discharging his duties with singular ability, he received in marriage the hand of the daughter of the celebrated Austrian Marshal Daun. At the time of John's death, Portugal was in a deplorable condition. Within, nothing but misery and distress, despite the immense wealth Brazil poured into the small kingdom; without, weakness and humiliation. For the Colonies of the East no longer existed, and those of the West produced wealth only to be poured into the hands of the English.

Counting upon the compliance of the king, and upon the obedience of his colleagues, he determined to use all the means in his power, and he did not hesitate to employ tyranny. His dictatorship lasted 30 years, but it was absolutely necessary. Portugal had to be saved in spite of herself.

His first care was to reanimate agriculture and industry, then almost abandoned. If he did not succeed in elevating the commerce of Portugal to its former height, he at least increased it to a great extent, by suppressing the pirates, by instituting two grand trading companies, and by introducing a new colonial system. The revenues next received his attention and soon felt the influence his masterly mind brought to bear on them. In that respect his first care was to abolish immunities as much as possible. He seized the royal estates that had been turned to the benefit of the great families of the kingdom.

But the most important of the edicts issued by the indefatigable minister, was the one in 1752, on the exportation of gold from Brazil. It was a blow aimed at the bonds by which England held the country, and although the influence exerted by the English annulled this patriotic design, great good was effected. At any rate he diminished the evil, if he could not destroy it.

During the dreadful earthquake which overthrew Lisbon on the morning of the 1st of November, 1755, thereby destroying 30,000 people and an incalcuable amount of property, Pombal showed himself worthy of the king's confidence. " To bury the dead, and help the living," constituted his first care. In the measures he took for the relief of the city, we see his wonderful promptness and genius, especially when he decided that an impost of $4\frac{1}{2}$ per cent. should be levied on all foreign merchandize.

Pombal did not refrain from attacking the Jesuits, whose power perhaps had become too great. In 1773, he succeeded in abolishing their institutions in Portugal, and in banishing them from the kingdom.

In 1762, Spain sent a force of 40,000 men into Tras-os-Montes, with a small body of French as auxiliaries. At first, success attended the efforts of the enemy, who captured Miranda, Braganza, Outeiro, Chaves, Freixel, Almeida and Villadelha But they were finally driven back with loss. Thus a great danger was passed in safety. Pombal attended to the organization of the army with such care, that, at the end of a few years, it consisted of 24 regiments of infantry, 12 of cavalry, and 4 of artillery.

Indeed the influence of Pombal was felt everywhere, at home and abroad. Prosperity once more returned to the kingdom. His power was absolute but salutary. Happy would Portugal have been, had his services been retained. But his severity had raised too many enemies against him. On the death of Joseph I, Pombal was left exposed to the storm raised by his enemies. The Queen, Dona Maria, felt constrained to sign a decree condemning him as a criminal to exile. Death soon released him from all further trouble.s Glorious as his services had been, his ministry was but a halt in the rapid decadence, which, for so many years, dragged this kingdom to ruin. The great projects he had conceived were abandoned; the code he had prepared remained unfinished; the Marine and the roads were neglected, and the finances, lately so flourishing, fell into their former condition.

The mental state of the queen having undergone in 1792, a serious alteration, her son, Prince of Brazil, D João Maria Joseph, assumed the reins of power, in 1799. D João, as regent, after having renewed the alliance with England, and seen himself badly seconded by her against Spain, endeavored to treat with Russia, and then with victorious France, with which country he desired to connect himself. The treaty of Badajoz (June 16th 1801) imposed on Portugal only the payment of a war indemity, and the cession of Olivenca to Spain. But after the rupture of the treaty of Amiens in 1806, the refusal of John to close his ports to the English vessels brought about the invasion of Portugal by a French corps d' armee under the orders of Junot, Duc d' Abrantes, and the Court of Lisbon, perceiving the uselessness of resistance, determined to embark for Brazil. It will be soon seen that the consequences of this departure, by which it was hoped to save the national unity on both sides of the Atlantic, were exactly what broke it.

Portugal was divided. The northern portion with Oporto as capital, was given to to the Infanta of Spain ; Algarves and Alem Tejo, Napoleon bestowed on the infamous Godoy, Prince of the Peace, as principalities, whilst the remaining districts, namely, Estremadura, Beira and Tras-os-Montes, remained in the hands of the emperor. Thus the all-powerful captain suppressed one of the oldest kingdoms in Europe. According to the words contained in the Imperial Moniteur, "The House of Braganza had ceased to reign." The royal family fled to Rio de Janerio. Junot, duc d' Abrantes, bearing the modest title of Governor General, was the true ruler.

· The Peninsular war brought about by the assistance of the English needs no description here. It will be sufficient to mention Junot, Soult and Massena, as the principal French commanders; and Wellington as the English leader. The result of the contest was the expulsion of the invader from Portugal. The French although driven forth, left behind them traces of their occupation. It was the same as in Germany,

Italy and all the countries into which the French troops penetrated. They had carried with them the new ideas resulting from
the Revolution, which ideas they left as an ineffaceable trace of
their stay. But although a great number of the young men
dreamt of establishing in their land, a government more worthy
of the age, the mass of the people did not understand these
theories. They rose to drive forth the foreigner, but political
liberty inspired them with only indifference.

John VI, refused to exchange Rio Janerio for Lisbon, and
adopted the new name of king of Portugal, Brazil, and Algarves. By his obstinacy he brought about a severance of the
ties that bound Brazil to Portugal.

* This absence of the regent, resulted in handing Portugal
over to England. Bresford had the honor of reorganizing the
army and of contending with it against the French. To him was
confided the government, which he carried on merely for the
benefit of his native land, England, although he owed all his
dignities to the unfortunate land which he ruled. The pro-
tectorate of France seemed to some, preferable to the ruinous
supremacy of their allies. At last, on the death of Dona Maria
in 1816, the regent became king under the name of John VI.

In 1821, an insurrection broke out in Oporto. The cause
of the insurrectionists was indeed the same as that of the nation.
Consequently it soon spread throughout the kingdom. In vain
were troops under General Vittoria and Count d' Amarante sent
against the rebels. All fraternised with the insurgents. Lisbon
took advantage of their absence to revolt. The new Junta
which met in that city, proclaimed the downfall of the regents,
and adopting as the basis of Portuguese liberty, the constitution
of Cadiz, it hastened to announce that the Cortes would be
called. Portugal was at length free. The desire for freedom
entered the hearts of the Brazilians, who thereupon rose in Para

---

* John did not assume the title of king during the lifetime of Dona Marie.

and in Pernambuco. John VI thus placed between two revolts, was constrained to yield to the wishes of his people, and
at the instance of his son, Dom Pedro, promised a constitution.
But the commission he appointed was composed of courtiers.
Perceiving this, again revolt lifted its head. Again was it ap-
peased by the promise of the king to confer his powers on Dom
Pedro, and by his announcing to the people that their desires ·
would be satisfied. John VI, shortly afterwards set sail for
Europe, leaving Brazil in charge of Dom Pedro.

Unlike Ferdinand VII, of Spain, who swore to maintain the
Spanish Charter only because he feared the consequences of a
refusal, the king of Portugal, disregarding the dangerous advice
of several to listen to the suggestions of " absolutists" Europe,
committed the care of drawing up the Portuguese constitution to
the Cortes, and when that was done, hastened to ratify it, imposing, at the same time, the oath upon the princes and dignitaries of the kingdom.

But the reformer committed the criminal blunder of endea-
voring to despoil Brazil of its rights and to reduce it to the rank
of a simple colony. Of course, the natural result followed.
Brazil, indignant at this injustice, rose up in anger to protest.
The chief of this powerful insurrection was Andrada, whose
family were paramount in the province of St. Paul.

On the 12th of October, 1822, the declaration of independence was proclaimed. Brazil became an empire under Don
Pedro. It was not until 1825, that her independence was acknowledged by the mother country. Shortly afterwards John
VI died, leaving as his direct heir, Dom Pedro. This prince
was recognized by all as king. Besides being the eldest son, he
was also Emperor of Brazil, and thus was in a position to re-
unite the two crowns. But the Infante Dom Miguel, his brother,
entertained secret hopes of mounting the European throne. A
large cortege of Portuguese dignitaries headed by the Duke of

Lafoés, embarked for Brazil, in order to carry to Dom Pedro the homage of his European subjects. On their arrival, in Rio Janeiro, it was found difficult to reign over the two countries. Dom Pedro at length determined to give his European States to his daughter Dona Maria, on the sole condition that she married her uncle, Dom Miguel. He had previously charged the English Ambassador, Lord Stewart, with a charter founded on the English and French Constitutions, for the Portuguese. The Queen, Isabella, was to retain the regency, with the Duke de Cadaval, the Patriarch of Lisbon, the Marquis de Vallada and the Count dos Arcos, as councillors.

However, a large number of the Portuguese consisting of the nobility and the clergy, with half of the rural population, protested against the charter, thereby throwing the regency into a state of confusion, from which it was drawn by General Saldanha. Saldanha being governor of Minho, had the charter sent to him, when he at once promulgated it throughout his districts. This conduct was imitated by all the other governors. The absolutists did not yield. An insurrection headed by the Count d' Amarante broke forth. Twice were the insurrectionists driven from the country. All in vain. They still maintained a bold front, and, being aided by Ferdinand VII, King of Spain, to whom the sight of a free nation existing as a neighbor was highly displeasing, they were enabled to present an indomitable obstacle to all the efforts of the government. At last Isabella asked for the assistance of England. By means of this timely help, the intestine agitation ceased for a time. Shortly afterwards, perceiving that troubles were about to recommence, Don Pedro transferred the regency to Don Miguel, in the hope that a man's hand would be sufficient to quell the disturbances. But Miguel excited by ambitious desires accepted the regency, intending to use it as a stepping stone to the crown. He left Vienna, in which city he had been sojourning, passed over to England where he received royal honors, and finally disembarked at Lisbon on the 22nd, of February, 1828, less as regent than as usurper. Two months sufficed for him to reach the end of his wishes. Pretending that, the entire nation had summoned him, he mounted the throne. Absoluteism wat at length triumphant, public liberty was at an end.

Dom Pedro, hearing of what had happened, repented that he had confided so generously, and in order to lessen the evil results of his misplaced confidence, he hastened to renew his abdication in favor of Dona Maria. This princess then sailed for Europe, intending to go to Vienna, and there await the march of events.

The Cortes confirmed the step taken by the usurper. But he was not recognized by Europe. Indeed the Portuguese Ambassador in London, Duke de Palmella, resigned his trust His example was followed by the other Portuguese diplomatist. But these protests made but little difference to Miguel. Palmella, Saldanha, Villaflon and others strove in vain to overthrow him. All were compelled to fly to Spain, and thence to England· Tyranny reigned supreme. Dona Maria, finding that only the island of Terceira, then the principal of the Azores, remained faithful to herself, went to England, in the hope of being able to gain the assistance of George III. She found, however, that no help was to be gained in that quarter. She determined to return to Brazil, there to await the hour of deliverance. In the meantime, Don Pedro had excited his Brazilian subjects against himself, by various mistakes, the chief of which was the favor he bestowed on the Portuguese Filisberto Caldeira The people compelled him to abdicate in favor of his son, Dom Pedro II. This step having met with entire success, he resolved to leave the country of which he had been emperor. During his voyage to Europe, he stopped at the island of San Miguel, one of the Azores, to encourage the adherents of his daughter, who were holding out there. Landing in England, he at once went to work, and so successfully, that, within a short time, he prepared two frigates, several smaller vessels and the munitions requisite for carrying on the war.

Louis Phillipe of France, also aided him to a great extent, by authorizing him to enlist recruits. The expedition consisting of about 300 English, 600 French, and as many Portuguese, on board several vessels, under the command of Sartorius, an English captain, set sail for the Azores. Having made himself complete master of these important islands, Dom Pedro made at once for Portugal, and landed at Villa du Condo, distant from Oporto about 14 miles. The reception of the new-comers was not encouraging. It was found necessary to retreat to Oporto, where they found warm friends, the people of that city having always been ardent lovers of liberty. The Miguelists hastened to beseige the place, as Pedro determined to remain there rather than expose his small army of voulunteers to a superior force in the open field, by marching on Lisbon. Cholera as well as the ravages of the sword devastated the camps of the usurper. What added to the joy of the besieged, was, the arrival on the 1st of January, 1833, of reinforcements accompanied by supplies, etc. These had been collected in London and in Paris. General Saldanha and Baron Solignac, both distinguished in the annals of the Napoleonic wars, assumed the direction of military matters, whilst Napier superintended the marine.

Instead of remaining within the walls of Oporto, Pedro determined to leave only a garrison in that city, and with the remainder of his troops, make a bold effort for victory. The Pedroists threw themselves against Álgarves, deceived Mollelos, who defended Alemtejo with 6000 militia, defeated Freitas under the walls of Setubal, and, masters of that city, arrived suddenly at Cacilhas, in front of Lisbon, on the opposite bank of the Sagus. Defeating the troops placed in front of Cacilhas, they thereby caused so much anxiety to the numerous garrison in Lisbon under the Duke de Cadaval that it evacuated the city and fled to Coimbra, and thence to the neighborhood of Oporto, which was being besieged by the usurper himself. Lisbon was occupied by the liberators on the following day. Oporto also witnessed the defeat of Don Miguel's troops. The way was now clear. Dona Maria quitted Paris and on Sept. 22nd, disembarked at Lisbon. There she recieved the crown from her father, who retained for himself only the title of regent, an office carrying with it a great deal of anxiety, since Don Miguel was even more formidable. This Prince, repulsed in his attempts on Lisbon, and driven from the strong lines, by which he threatened the capitol, was compelled to retreat to Santaren, where he was immediately besieged by Saldanha and Terceira. But the death of Ferdinand VII, who was the most important aid to absolutism in the Peninsula, struck a fatal blow at Don Miguel's cause.

The selecting of Dona Isabella, instead of Don Carlos, as his successor, was also a great misfortune, for the usurper Don Carlos came to Santarem less as an allied sovereign than as a fugitive. To add to the approaching storm, a corps of Spanish troops passed the frontier in order to watch over the plots that might be directed against Isabella.

What could Don Miguel do against such odds, especially when France, England, Spain and Portugal, formed a quadruple allinace? Unable to escape, he threw himself into Evora, where he was quickly enveloped by the forces under Saldanha and Terceira. On the the 26th of May, 1834, he surrendered. The struggle was at an end, Dona Maria was sole sovereign.

The regent Dom Pedro, worn out by fatigue, felt the approach of death. He hastened to call a council, and presented to it several great reforms. To assure public peace, he abdicated the regency, declared Dona Maria of age, and gave to her as husband, Duke of Luchtehenberg, son of Eugene Beauharnais.

Then having done all that the world required of him, he occupied himself with the repose of his soul. He died September 24th, 1834.

At length Dona Maria reigned, but it was with some difficulty. Hardly had her father breathed his last, when tha Cortes became agitated, the clubs intrigued, the absolutists took fresh courage, the vanquishing party divided, and Don Miguel dreamt of regaining the crown. The anarchy of the kingdom had increased to such an extent, that this prince startled Europe, by suddenly departing from Vienna and entering the kingdom. But owing to the active measures taken by England, with the consent of the other powers composing the quadruple alliance, the crown was assured to the queen, and the attempt of her uncle failed.

The principal ministers of Dona Maria were Palmella, Freire and Carralho, men of great ability. They were unable however skillful they might be, to avoid recurring to the usual expedients of meeting a deficit, viz: the sale of public property, loans, etc. Even then they did not succeed in paying the public functionaries, or in making up the deficit. The army, the marine and the credit of Portugal fell into the deplorable condition to be expected after 30 years of war and anarchy.

The liberals, who were the enemies of the ministry, attributed these misfortunes to the cabinet, and not to the real causes. The ministry perceiving this, redoubled their efforts to place the affairs of the kingdom on a solid basis, and to silence their enemies. The opposition still continued. It was found necessary to repress several emcute in the streets. A crisis was iminent; when news arrived of the celebrated conspiracy of la Graufa in Spain.

The natural consequences of the check Christina met with soon followed. The movement produced in Madrid, had its counter movement in Lisbon. The clubs became excited, the secret societies armed, and the opposition threatened. Despite the dissolution of the Cortes by Dona Maria, the ministry fell, and the queen was compelled to accept Bernard de Sâ, Lumia res, and Passos, as her advisers. These latter set to work in a vigorous manner, to introduce more advanced ideas of civilization and of reform. The queen endeavored to excite a counter revolution, but, although she had the assistance of the squadrons commanded by Lord Paget and by Admiral Hugore, her attempt failed.

The fall of Passos and the concessions made by the Cortes did not pacify the queen, enraged at the failure of her attempt. Again revolt raised its head. The Baron de Leiria, soon joined by Saldanha and Tericia, excited an insurrection in the northern provinces, under the cry of "viva carta." There was no doubt that the queen was engaged in this affair. But the Cortes affected to be ignorant of this complicity, and invested Mon. de Bomfine and de Sa with extraordinary powers to repress the insurgents. The forces were equal. A long civil war seemed to be on the point of breaking out, when the corps d'armie, which Dona Maria had sent to the assistance of Isabella of Spain, under the command of Viscount das Antas, made its appearance, and settled the question, by declaring against the chartists, and by beating them at Ruivaens.

A new ministry was formed and was composed of Das Antas the conqueror at Ruivaens as chief, and of Mon. de Bomfine and de Sâ. One remarkable circumstance should be noticed in this place. It is that, during all the troubles to which the kingdom was a prey for so long a period, one thing remained unchanged, it was the prestige of royalty. A beneficial prestige, since, it preserved Portugal from complete anarchy and chaos.

The Portuguese had an opportunity of displaying their vigor to Spain, who haughtily demanded the liberty of the Douro. All the parties united for the purpose of refusing the summons of Spain. They protested so plainly that the danger, which threatened to destroy them served only to prove their strength. Espartero, the Spanish regent, soon withdrew his demand. England having countenanced Portugal in this refusal, thought it was a good opportunity to request a renewal of the Methuen treaty. But her request was made in vain. Taught by the 130 years of misery, resulting, from the treaty, the Portuguese were unwilling to enter into the same trap.

In 1842, the Minister of Justice, M. Costa Cabral, aided by the King, Ferdinand de Saxe Cobourg, second husband of the queen, and by others of high rank, went to Coimbra and proclaimed the abolition of the established constitution. He was successful. Sustained by the protection of the Court, by the servility of the two chambers, and by the friendship of his brother, the Governor of Lisbon, and by the kindly neutrality of Miguelists, M. de Costa Cabral, had at first no difficulty to meet with in regard to the parties. But he soon found the annual deficit, the increasing debt, the wretched condition of the army and navy, and the impoverishment of the people to be difficulties of great magnitude. Some steps which he took for the amelioration of public affairs were wise; but they were not enough. Popular discontent continued. His enemies took advantage of the dissatisfaction caused by a new tax, to incite the inhabitants of the province of Minho to revolt. Their example was followed all over the kingdom; and the minister found it necessary to fly from the kingdom with his brother. His enemies then stepped into power.

They did not remain in power very long. The queen, aided by France, England and Spain, soon contrived to overthrow them. Costa Cabral was recalled. His reception was most flattering. Having modestly refused the ministry, he offered to invest the Marshal Duke de Saldanha, with the office. But his offer was declined by the Marshal, and also by the Duke de Terceira and by M. Duarto Leitao. Nothing remained for him, but to accept it himself. He at the same time received the title of Count de Thomar. The new president of the council, used his power to correct abuses, to unite Portugal and Rome, to ameliorate the state of finances, to raise up commerce and agriculture, and to reanimate the marine.

But he soon encountered opposition. His former adversaries, disconcerted by the promptness of his return and by his unexpected success, renewed their intrigues. The great lords offended by his supremacy, the journalists angered by the severities of press laws, brought forward in 1850, the Miguelists, disgusted with his reforms, and others converted into enemies from one cause or another, all combined to overthrow him despite the majority he had in the Cortes. A cheif was found in the person of the Duke de Saldhana. At first the duke had been the aid of the Count de Thomar. But constancy and fidelity are not characteristic of that personage. Incited by a slight he had received, he threw himself into the ranks of the opposition. He declared war, by virulent attack on the war minister. England, at the instigation of Lord Palmerston, assisted the factious parties, and by a judicious expenditure of money, brought affairs to a condition satisfactory to herself. The Duke de Saldanha continued in his attacks. To be prime minister, or to be chief of the opposition constituted the continual alternative in which he passed his life. According to a newspaper, "O Patriota," he had already changed his opinions fifty-four times. But his interests were always paramount, and now, aided by England, who saw an opportunity of refastening the bonds, which had almost ruined Portugal, he was enabled to present a bold front. Although he met with some reverses, he succeeded in overthrowing his patriotic adversary. The Count de Thomar was banished and the Duke de Saldanha reigned in his stead. The fall of the former had been accllerated by the ruin of the Spanish Premier Marshal Narvaez, who had been in accord with him. Only a few days after Narvaez fell, Saldanha succeeded in inducing two battalions to revolt. Oporto was the first to rebel, then Coimbra, and finally Lisbon, in which city, a leader was found in the person of Sylva Cabral, a brother of the prime minister. Dona Maria was compelled to accede to all the demands made by the discontented insurrectionists, and she had the mortification of seeingthe Duke de Saldanha, enter Lisbon amid the applause of an admiring populace.

The ministry was composed of the Marshals, Rodriguez da Fonseca Magalhaes, Antonio Maria de Fontes, Pereira de Mello, (at present President of the Ministerial Council,) Ierois d' Althoneguia, Almeida Garret, and Antonio Luiz de Sleabra. The chief of the ministry was Fonseca Magalhaes, a venerable and enlightened man, who was assisted principally by M. Fontes de Mello. The latter inaugurated a new epoch of progress, of which there was a great need. M. Fontes was composed of the stuff, proper for a statesman, with broad and decisive views. Undoubtedly he was somewhat hasty in his measures, but his colleague Fonseca Magalhaes endeavored to moderate this patriotic ardor. It is to M. Fontes that the country is indebted for the first railroads. The public attention was too much engaged with political theories, to spare time for such vital questions, as concerned roads, rail-ways, telegraph lines, agricultural schools, the re-establishment of finance, the organization of the army and navy, the improvement of the colonial administration, the reform of the academy of science, the preparation of codes (civil and penal) and in fine all the other objects, which political discords had hitherto caused to be neglected.

The death of Dona Maria, which resulted from an unfortunate accouchment, 15 Nov., 1853, made no change in public affairs. Her husband Don Ferdinand II, acting as regent to D. Pedro V (still under age,) retained in office, the Saldhana Magulhars ministry. The queen was very much regretted; daughter of the soldier-king Dom Pedro IV, placed upon the throne after the most heroic efforts of the liberators, she inspired the highest respect as queen, on account of her firm and courageous character. The regent contributed on his side to the task of calming political passions, and of directing the energies of his ministers to the developement of industrial works, which are one of the principal sources of modern civilization, and which were in a backward condition in Portugal. The fusion of the political parties was effected by the choice of capable men for the various offices, without regard to past politics. Thus émentes became impossible. The Portuguese civil wars in this manner received their death-blow, and thenceforward under the protection of a peace which has lasted to the present day, both within and without, Portugal entered upon a series of measures which were calculated to bring her to a state of prosperity. We can ascertain the better what Portugal has gained since that memorable epoch, by means of statistics and the logical deductions made in the proper place, than through the most brilliant and the most abstract oratorica-declamations. When we touch on the commerce, the agriculture, and the finances of this kingdom as it stands at present, it will be easy, by means of comparison, to judge of the real progress.

During the reign of Dona Maria II, Charles Albert, who had sought refuge in Portugal, after having abdicated on the unfortunate field of Novara, in favor of his son Victor Emmanuel, died in Oporto. He had chosen as his asylum, that city, which had always been the impregnable bulwarks of Portuguese liberty.

Although the King Ferdinand retained the Saldanha-Magalhaes ministry in power, he was, after a short period, compelled to replace it with that of the Marquis de Loulé, who, in his turn, gave way to the Terceira cabinet. Dom Pedro V, eldest son of Dona Maria II, 30th King of Portugal, and 26th of Algarves, recei-

(4)

ved the power from the hands of his father, the regent, on the
16th of September 1855, after a visit he had made to the Courts
of France, England, Germany and Italy.

The Duke de Terceira organized a ministry, composed of
Fontes, Casal Ribeiro, Serpa, Ferreri, and Ferrao, and he himself retained the portfolios of war and of foreign affairs. This administration, as well as those immediately preceding it, preserved
more or less, the character and spirit of conciliation, it maintained also the fusion of parties, introduced by Fonseca Magalhaes. The incoming ministers devoted their attention to the
various improvements in roads, telegraphs, etc., so necessary to
the well-being of a country.

The cholera, yellow fever, and a sad dispute with France,
concerning the ship "Charles and George," which had been
seized by the Portuguese, on the east coast of Africa, because of its
infraction of the slave-laws, were unfortunate events, which caused
much affliction to the young king, Dom Pedro V, in the beginning of his reign. Dom Pedro displayed considerable courage
and resignation in the midst of these troubles.

Public instruction interested him deeply, and he founded in his
Château de Mafra, a school, over which he watched with great
care. He abandoned $30,000 of his modest civil list, in order
to create Professorships of national and foreign literature in the
academy of sciences at Lisbon. Dom Pedro married in 1858,
Princess Stephanie, daughter of Prince Charles of Hohenzollern
Sigmaringro. This amiable princess expired after a short illness
on the 17th of July, 1859, regretted by the Portuguese. Her
cultivated mind, religious and charitable tendencies, together
with her sweet character explain the cause of this regret.

The unfortunate Dom Pedro V, did not long survive the one
whom he adored with his whole soul, on the 11th of November
1861, he died, from a typhoid fever he had acquired during a
chase at Villa Vicosa.

The present head of the state, his next brother, succeeded him immediately. He married on the 16th of October 1862, Princess Maria Pia de Savoy, daughter of Victor Emmanuel.

Dom Louis I, is endowed with qualities, which are indispensable to a constitutional king, and he is thereby bound more closely to the destinies of the nation.

We have determined to go no father in this historical aperçu as it wonld not be wise to enter into the history of the recent events, owing partly to the inconsistent reports received. Sufficient has been placed before the reader to give some idea of the history of Portugal, and to enable him to enter upon a perusal of the succeeding articles, with a certain degree of interest, as well as of ability to understand them.

LANGUAGE AND LITERATURE.

WHILST proposing to give an idea concerning our literature, we deem it just to state at once, that Portugal indeed has a literature to itself; as Sismonde de Sismondi has it, her language instead of becoming a dialect of the Castilian, has been looked upon by that independent people as a mark of their sovereignty, and it has been cultivated with zeal. The distinguished men, whom Portugal has produced, have endeavored to give to their country all the branches of literature; they have essayed every branch, in order that they might not leave any advantage to their neighbors, and the national spirit has given to their productions a character that is "quite different from that of Castilian compositions."

The history of the Portuguese language is naturally bound up with the history of the race, since at each invasion of the Peninsula, by foreign colonies or by foreign armies, the language then spoken must have undergone considerable alterations. The colonies established on the coast brought their ideas, and commingled them in course of time by the communications of commerce. The various strangers, who visited the ports, must have had great influence in moulding the tongue The words of Greek, Phoenician, Celtic, Iberian and Carthaginian origin which are found in the Portuguese and Castilian languages indicate this sufficiently.

It would be useless to discuss the question as to what was the language generally spoken at the epoch when the Romans, endeavored to subject the Peninsula to their sway. The absence of decisive proofs renders it too perplexing a point to admit of a solution. The rare vestinges of those times indicate rather a mélange of all the tongues introduced into the Peninsula than the predominance of a single one.

The influence of the institutions and of the laws introduced by the Romans became permanent, and, after the complete conquest of the country, we find that the general language must have been only Latin. Christianity employed that tongue in its services and especially in the preaching of the gospel. In fact the Spaniards not only employed Latin as the general and usual tongue; they even gave to Roman literature such men as Seneca and Lucan.

Although the Arabs conquered the country, no radical changes were effected, as these benign conquerors allowed the subjugated races to retain their customs, religion, and laws. Latin thus escaped this new danger. It remained the official and religious language, whilst Arabic and Hebrew languages, (which latter had been brought into the country by the Jew) served for industry, art, poetry and science.

When Portugal declared herself independent, the Court of Leon spoke the Galician, which language was employed by the Portuguese; but posterior events determined its decadence and favored the developement of the Castilian and the formation of Portuguese. The Court of Leon adopted the Castilian, and, although the poets still continued to use Galician, the new language of the court triumphed over and replaced it. The independence of Portugal, the aversion of the Portuguese to the Galicians, and the wars with the Castilians, insensibly drew away the subjects of Alphonse I, from each of those two languages, and created the Portuguese idiom. The Galician becme an obscure and unimportant dialect in Spain, whereas Portuguese was formed by civilization and the energy of a free spirit, it marked

its place among the European languages toward the end oft he
13th century.

French and Provençal also have contributed to the formation
of Portuguese.

It is generally supposed that Spanish and Portuguese are
only two dialects of the same language, and people can scarcely
conceive how these two peoples, whose political organizations
were made under almost identical conditions, do not speak the
same language.

The influence of the Celtic, Greek, Phoenician and Carthaginian origins, and the action of the Latin and Hebrew, having
been the same with the Portuguese and the Spaniards, there was
not for a long period, any material change in the constitutional
principles of the two languages; during the first part of the
monarchy of Alphonse I. Portuguese did not differ from Spanish to any great extent; the differences which now separate them
are only the consequence of the modifications occasioned by the
opposite directions which the two nations had to give to their
activity.

Whereas the Spaniards, on account of their frequent contact
with the French, and their exploits in Italy, their occupation of
the low countries, and their relations with Austria, were forced
to admit of more or less foreign influence in the idiomatic construction of their language, the Portuguese, by their isolation in
Europe and by their conquest in distant lands, remained faithful to their Latin origin. For the same reasons, the Arabic
vestiges are purer in Portugal than in Spain, although the
Spaniards have always retained the guttural sounds of " J " and
of " X," an Arabism quite unknown in Portugal. There are
many Arabic words preserved in Portugal, which have ceased
to be employed in Spanish. The two languages adopted the
word " alfaiate " (tailor) : the Spaniards used it up to the 15th
and 16th centuries. The Portuguese use it now, but the Span-

iards have replaced it with "sastre," from the Italian "sartore." Other examples could be cited.

Portuguese is rich in words, varied constructions, synonyms, derivatives, words signifying a single action and in expressions often untranslatable. Its pronunciation is sweet without the breathings to be found in French and in Northern tongues, and without the guttural sounds which are found so difficult in Spanish and German. It combines the concision of Latin with the copious abundance of Oriental tongues ; and without being severe like the Spanish, it is freer in its adornments than the French, and more serious than the Italian, of which it possesses the harmony and the sweetness.

There are, however, some serious defects, the use of diphthongs at the end of words and the nasal dissonance in " ao," (pronounced " aon "), add nothing to the beauty and the euphony of Portugese. As the Royal Academy of Sciences has not gone far in the dictionary it is preparing, all questions in regard to the language must be decided by citations from the Classic writers of the XVI century. The orthography has no fixed rules, a want which is often felt.

Science and literature have always found a welcome in Portugal from the very time that the monarchy was established, up to the present day. Alphonse Henriques, the first King of the Portuguese had as tutor, a poet, Egas Moniz, whose verses are yet extant. The Arabian and the Jewish savants always received protection from the Christian monarchs of their times. Denis I and his natural son, D. Pedro, possessed that attribute, so common to men of an exalted genius, a love of letters.

But it is not till we reach the 2nd dynasty that we come to the Augustan age of Portuguese literature. It was during the time of voyages and discoveries, of the introduction of printing and of the perfecting of the Portuguese language, that we find the epoch of the creation of a literature that would be worthy

of the most advanced nations in Europe. What a galaxy of
brilliant names! Vasco de Gama and Alphonse d'Albuquerque ;
King D. Duarte, the eloquent; Camœns, Ferreira, Gil Vicente,
Sâ de Miranda and Bernardim Ribeiro ; Fernao Losses,
Azurara, Joao de Barros and D. Jeronimo Osorio ; Gran Vasco
and the Hollandas ; the Infante D. Henri, Pedro Nunes and
D. Joao de Castro, are names that will live for ever.

The 15th century, the heroic age of Portugal, beheld the
blossoming of the flower of Portuguese poetry, the romances for
which productions Castilian literature was also noted. The
Portuguese " Cancioneiros " of that period are richer than those
of the same kind to be found in contemporaneous Spanish
literature. Unfortunately, Portuguese poetry, which was especially poetry for a Court, neglected nature, and, in course of
time, became idyllic, insipid and destitute of originality.

The dramatic art, although occupying but a secondary rank
in Portuguese literature, has the incontestable merit of a
priority which she shares with only the native land of Trissin.
Sa de Miranda, who lived from 1495 to 1558, and his contem-
porary, Gil Vicente, were the predecessors of the two illustrious Spaniards, Copé de Vega and Calderon. Antonio
Ferreira (1528–1569), surnamed the Horace of Portugal, on
account of his lyrics, was the author of the national tragedy of
Inez de Castro, as well as of a comedy, the " Jealous." But the
man, who alone ought to be considered as having erected an
immortal monument to Portuguese literature was Luiz de
Camoens, born in 1524, whom the " Lusiades " places in the
rank of the glorious epic poets, Homer, Virgil and Milton.
Not one of the succeeding poets inherited any of his genius.
Soon the old taste for pastoral poetry invaded the literature
anew, and spread itself during the 17th century, in a deluge of
sonnets. The Spanish domination completed the literary decadence of the country.

It is true, that the new national dynasty, in the 18th century, gave some encouragement to letters. In 1720, John V founded the " Academy of Portuguese History," and in 1757, was created, under the name of Arcadia, another academy, which lasted till 1776. About the same time the works of the great French writers were in the ascendant in Portugal, and drove out the Italian tastes, which had lasted for so long a period. But the effects were only superficial. There was a reaction from the old bucolic taste, thanks to the united efforts of all the intelligent men of the present literary epoch ; but this reaction, at first, brought in merely a crowd of translations from the ancient and the modern languages, and some weak imitations of foreign models.

We meet with the first specimens of prose in the chronicles of the 14th century. But this kind of writing remained in an un-improved condition, until the 15th and the 16th centuries, after the " Renaissance." Fernao Lopes' chronicle of John I. is a proof of this improvement. Those two centuries were very pro-lific in romances of chivalry, some of the most celebrated of which belong to Portugal. Amadis de Gaul is the best known. Among the historians, the first to acquire reputation was Joao de Barros, whose " Asia " (1552,) continued by Diogo de Couto, is even at the present day the best guide in regard to the history of the Portuguese discoveries in that part of the world. The heroic age of the nation was specially treated by Fernao Lopes de Castanheda, by the celebrated Alphonse d'Albuquerque, in his commentaries, and lastly by Damiao de Goes, in his Chron-icle of Emmanuel, the Fortunate.

A new era opened in 1833, when temporal absolutism in the person of D. Miguel was abolished. Although the masses have not yet displayed many signs of increasing intelligence, the élite of the nation have felt the benign influences of the Goddess of Liberty. Among the men that have pointed out the way for advance, there are two who are remarkable for several reasons; the Viscount D'Almeida Garret and Alexander Herculano de Carvalho. The former, a brilliant poet, minister, diplomatist and orator, died in 1854. As familiar with the works of the French and of the Italian muse, as with the best traditions of the ancient national poetry, he displayed a great superiority in romance and in lyric productions. Garret alone constituted a literature. He was the author of the Romancero, Adozinda and Dona Branca, the graceful lyric badinage Retrato de Venus, the humorous "Travels in my Country," the tragedies Cato and Meropus, and the national dramas Auto de Gil bicente, Frey Luiz de Sousa, and Arco de Sant'Arnna.

Herculano is also a writer of similar universality. His writings are stamped with the mark of sadness. His " A voz de propheta," Eurico, O monge de Cister, and "The Establishment of the Portuguese Inquisition" are of a surpassing merit. We cannot do more than mention the names of Rebello da Silra, Mendes Leal, Andrade Corvo, Camillo Castello Branco, Bulhão, Pato, Antonio Pereira da Cunha, and A. Feliciamo de Castilho. Two poems entitled "A noite do Castello" and "Os Cuimes do bardo," by Castilho, are gems in regard to sentiment and style.

Enough has been said to show that we should not regard Portugal as a disinherited country in a literary point of view. There exists a literary class, which, despite many annoying disadvantages, has produced much. What is wanted is the serious attention of a public more numerous and less indifferent than the one for which it is obliged to work at present. It is to be hoped that time, the great healer, will not hesitate to come to the assistance of Portuguese literature. A new era has opened. Patience alone is necessary.

Political Organization.

The government of Portugal is monarchical, hereditary and representative. The Constitutional Charter drawn up by Dom Pedro IV, April 29th, 1826, at Rio Janeiro, and amended by the additional act of July 5th, 1852, is the fundamental law of the kingdom. It is divided into 8 sections, containing 145 articles; 1st of the territorial state of the Monarchy, and the established church; 2d of the Portuguese nationality and naturalization; 3d of the distinctions in regard to the national powers and representation; 4th of the chambers and the electoral system; 5th of royalty; 6th of the judicial power; 7th of the provincial and financial administration; 8th, finally, of the general guaranties in reference to the liberty and rights of citizens. It is at once a constitutional law and a programme of excellent principles which require only a strict adherence, to produce good results.

The King bears the title of "Very Faithful Majesty, by the grace of God, King of Portugal and of Algarves of this side and the other side of the sea, in Africa, Lord of Guinea, of the conquest, navigation and commerce of Ethiopia, Arabia, Persia and India."

The national colors placed by Don Pedro, in the white flag of the ancient monarchy, are blue and white vertically divided, with the royal arms in the centre of the standard.

The heir apparent of the crown, formerly called "Prince of Brazil," takes the title of "prince royal," and his first-born that of "Prince of Beira." Both are termed Royal Highnesses. The

person of the sovereign is, constitutionally, irresponsible, inviolable and sacred. His majority is fixed by the charter at 18
years. He is forbidden to absent himself from the kingdom
without having first obtained the consent of the Cortes. The
husband of the reigning queen has no part in the government
and assumes the title of king only after he has had a son or
daughter. He may, however, be invested with the regency
during the heir's minority. The civil list allowed the present
sovereign, Don Luiz I, amounts to about $400,000. The Court
is maintained on as simple a scale as possible, consisting of
comparatively few officers, the ruinous expenditures in the reign
of John V having taught a lesson in that respect which will
never be forgotton. The officers are as follows: Grand-maitre
de la cour, Marshal Duke de Saldanha, Grand-aumonier, Patriarch of Lisbon, Grand-écuyer, Duke de Loulé, Grand-mâitre des
cérémonies, Count de Rio Maior, Intendant (Administrador da
fazenda,) Councillor S. do Conto e Castro Marcarenhas, first
aide-de-comp to the king, General of Division, Marquis de Sâ da
Bandeira.

The Portuguese Charter recognizes 4 powers ; the legislative
power, divided between the 2 chambers (who make, interpret,
suspend and abrogate the laws), and the king (who sanctions
or rejects them) ; the moderator and the executive power,
both constituting the basis of the royal power ; lastly, the power
bestowed on the independent magistrates and on the jury, who
exercise it in the name of the sovereign. The king and the
assembly-general of the cortes form the national representation. The cortes consists of two chambers, one of
Peers and the other of Deputies. Head of the state, the king
alone is invested with the executive power, as well as with the
moderating power. By virtue of the last, he may convoke ex-
traordinarily the cortes, or prorogue them, create new peers and
dissolve, if he thinks proper, the elective chamber, with the sav-

ing clause, that he must order new elections to replace it. He nominates and renominates his ministers, can suspend them from their functions (the magistrates being exceptions to this rule), and he has the privilege of pardoning and of granting an amnesty.

The executive power is exercised through the medium of his ministers, acting under the ordinary conditions of a parliamentary regime, and assisted by a council of state, the members of which are nominated for life by the sovereign. The king is invested with the command of the forces by land and sea ; he may declare war or make peace ; and, treating with foreign powers, he directs the external politics. But according to the 10th Article of the Additional Act, he must have the approbation of the cortes, when negotiating treaties, conventions and concordats. He is the dispenser of all honors, dignities and pardons, and confers not only the diplomatic, consular, magisterial and political posts, but also the bishoprics and other ecclesiastical appointments.

The charter guarantees to all citizens equality before the law, but without prejudice to the titles and other honorary privileges belonging to the nobility. All the Portuguese without distinction, are admissible to the public functions, as well as to military and naval appointments. Individual liberty, the security of persons and of property, the inviolability of domicile and of letters are also guaranteed, as well as the right of petition and the liberty of the press. But the rules and formalities, the observation of which determines the ordinary safeguard of these liberties, can be, in virtue of a reserve in the final article of the same charter, suspended by the government as well as by the chambers, in the cases where the safety of the state demands it. These suspensions have been numerous, especially during the tempests of Maria's reign.

The chamber of deputies is renewed every 4 years. The

legislative sessions are annual and commence of the 2d of January. Although the legal duration is determined at 3 months, it is as a rule prolonged beyond that time, according to the number and the importance of subjects for deliberation. The labors of the peers commence and end at the same time as those of the deputies. There are 107 deputies. To be eligible for the office, a certain revenue, minimum of which is fixed at 400,000 reis, (about $400,) must be enjoyed by the candidate, although from this law the following are exempt, viz: officers of the army and navy, priests, doctors, and in general, all those who have completed a superior course of education. Every citizen, possessing a revdnue of at least 100,000 reis, (or $100,) is a voter. The above mentioned exceptions hold good in this case also ; indeed, all who have diplomas of a superior or secondary education may vote.

The initiative in regard to supplies, etc., belongs exclusively to the chamber of deputies, and that chamber alone can decree the right of indicting the ministers and councillors of the state.

The number of peers is unlimited. They are nominated for life and the dignity is hereditary. To be admitted by right of succession, one must be 25 years of age at least, and possess a certificate of good conduct signed by 3 peers. The conditions of a good education and of an intelligent capacity must also be fulfilled.

There are seven ministers ; they are those of the interior, of the finances, of justice and public worship, of war, of tne navy and the colonies, of foreign affairs, of public works, commerce and industry.

The abolition of the death penalty for political crimes is one of the dispositions of the additional Act. Since the promulga tion of that act, it has been abolished, for even civil crimes, and it exists only in the military code.

Roman Catholicism is the state religion, but all the other

sects are tolerated in Portugal, with this sole restriction, they may not be publicly celebrated in temples possessing the characteristic exterior of religious edifices.

The judiciary power is untrammeled, and is composed of judges and juries as in England, the United States, etc. The judges are nominated for life, and may not be dispossessed of office, except by a judicial sentence.

Justice is administered by the various courts, from which an appeal can be made to a superior tribunal, endowed with the functions similar to those of the U. S. Supreme Court.

In regard to administrative organization, Portugal is divided into two distinct parts, the kingdom proper with the adjacent islands, and the colonies beyond the sea. The latter division is under the jurisdiction of the minister of " Marine and Colonies." The kingdom proper, with Madeira and the Azores, will be found to consist of 21 departments. These departments are directed by a magistrate called " Civil Governor," who is appointed by the king. Without enumerating all his duties, we may say that this official is the centre of the departmental administration ; his power is exercised over all the branches of the public service, and extends, in cases of emergency, to the adoption of extraordinary and dictatorial measures, according to the gravity of the circumstances. Of course he must submit all his plans for the approbation of the government.

A few remarks concerning some of the defects in the political organization of Portugal might not be considered inopportune.

Most of the ministers that have succeeded one onother in Portugal have recognized the necessity of a reform in our administration. That this reform has not already been brought about, is to be attributed chiefly to the resistance of the nation, and of the interests that have been begotten from the natural disposition of the people, which obstacles are always encountered by modern science and innovation.

The proposition which was recently presented to the cortes by the minister of the interior, A. Rodrigues Sampayo, contains the project of establishing the administrative organization on a new basis. She proposes to create a local political life, which has hitherto been but little developed ; to establish the government of the people by themselves, by means of popular suffrage ; to confide to the elective bodies the management of their interests; to educate and prepare the citizens progressively for assuming the duties connected with the general administration of the state, and finally to relieve the central government from occupying itself with interests, the protection of which could be confided more advantageously to the Superior District Courts, founded by popular vote. In a word, in the proposed plan of reform, the principle of decentralising is paramount and is instigated by the necessity of bringing forth those adjuncts, so indispensable to the life of a nation, which undoubtedly appears to be governed by liberal ideas.

One of the great difficulties encountered in the various branches of the public administration, is found in the general disposition of the nation. The initiative must always be taken by the executive, when the performance of any work not immediately connected with the management of public affairs, is demanded. The people always wait for the action of the government.

In absolute monarchies, it is logical to expect that all should look toward the central administration when anything is to be projected, but the theory is inapplicable to a country governed by institutions which have national sovereignty for base.

The great defect to which we allude will disappear before the light which already penetrates into the minds of the Portuguese. Undoubtedly the great obstacle to the introduction of the democratic doctrine, will be found in the natural indolence, and in a certain indifference which so effects the Portuguese that they desire to be governed rather than to take the reins of government into their own hands. However, when an error is recognized, there is also a manifest desire to correct it. It is not sufficient that the laws of a country should be good; the faithful execution of them is equally important. They should be binding one very one.

The privilege,which some public functionaries enjoy, of not being accused, in the civil or the criminal courts, about their official conduct, should be abolished. It is one of the points demanded by the reform. This question, with that of enlarging the popular suffrage constitute two of the most important articles in the proposed administrative code.

Thus this code creates decentralisation on a large scale, and contains many salutary innovations. Let us hope that it will be realized, despite the opposition offered by several districts. Developed for public utility and without party-spirit, it will mark a great step in the progress and happiness of the people, and will overthrow the system of centralisation, which has been for so long a time, an obstacle in the public affairs of Portugal..

ETHNOGRAPHY.

If we pass from the country to the inhabitants, we shall find that the population of Portugal offers nearly the same character as that of Spain, with at least, one single aboriginal element, the Basque. But the mélange of races is more strongly apparent in the former than in the latter, although it occupies only a small portion of the Peninsula. The blood of the ancient Lusitanians was mixed with that of all the nations, which, whether as conquerors or as conquered, have occupied the country; Carthagenians, Romans, German tribes, French of the feudal ages, Arabs and Jews. The influence of the Moorish element upon the mass of the people has not been less marked than in the neighboring kingdom. Cut off by its position from the rest of Europe, Portugal retains in many rural districts, the types of the original inhabitants. In fact, their own character and physiognomy have been retained unchanged.

The Portuguese are, in general, endowed with a great deal of kind-heartedness. They are susceptible to impressions and capable of courageous sacrifices; their lively and sensitive character sometimes carries them away, but rancor never burns within their breasts. Although they have been accused of being vindictive, an impartial observer would perceive that such is not the case. Despite their penchant for ideas of liberty and of civic equality, they are fond of honorary distinctions, such as decorations and titles of nobility, to which, by the way, all meritorious citizens in Portugal may aspire, no matter what their social origin may be. Lately, these destinctions were distributed somewhat profusely, and their value, which depends upon a discriminating choice combined with parsimony, became a little depreciated.

The Portuguese are of small stature, and possess a dark complexion. Their eyes and hair are black, although numerous exceptions to this rule are to be found in the north. If they are not distinguished for regularity of features, or for elegance of form, they are, as a rule, robust, sober, capable of bearing privation and fatigue.

The Portuguese ladies are always accompanied, during their promenades, by a domestic, and it is impossible to do away with this custom, just now, owing to various causes. They take very little exercise, the want of which injures their health as well as complexion. It is to be hoped that more healthy and civilized habits will be adopted. Then in Portugal, as in the United States and elsewhere, woman will be at liberty to go wheresoever she pleases, assured beforehand of the respect and consideration of every one.

I cannot say, notwithstanding my regret, that the Portuguese women are, in general, as handsome as the American; but in Beira some remarkable specimens of female beauty are to be met with. A brunette complexion, teeth of an unequalled whiteness, magnificent hair, and black eyes, filled with expression, distinguish many of the Portuguese women. Their height, it is true, is not always graceful, and their walk might be less stiff in style. They dress themselves with elegance for soirées, etc., but their toilette in the morning, and for the promenade, is not always in the best taste. In this respect they have much to learn from the American ladies. Although the women have been reproached with possessing a lax morality, they are, in general, good and affectionate mothers, and they have, at times, proved their devotion in a remarkable manner.

Some writers, who have been struck by the Hebrew type of the inhabitants in various parts, assert that the Jews were the progenitors of the Portuguese. In this, they err. True, that type is frequently met with, but only in isolated places. The reason is, that, owing to the comparatively mild laws of Portugal in regard to the persecuted Jews, these unfortunate outcasts sought shelter in that country. They have undoubtedly exerted great influence, but no greater than was to be expected from the numbers that made Portugal their home.

Whilst speaking about the reception of the Jews by the Portuguese, it would not be amiss to mention that hospitality reigns supreme in Portugal. The stranger is certain of a warm welcome.

We should not conceal the fact, that vanity somewhat tarnishes the lustre of the brilliant qualities of the Portuguese. It is a defect, which, it is pretended, is to be attributed to race and climate, and which is excited and maintained by the reaction against the loss of their political importance. Brought up in the traditions of a glorious past, and emerging from the most difficult tests, without losing either liberty or independence the Portuguese support with difficulty the raillery of their detractors, and, whilst waiting for what the future must bring in exchange for their efforts of regeneration and of progress, they recall their former power in order to strengthen their perseverance and to impose upon their adversaries.

It is easy to find among the Portuguese, faithful and devoted friends as well as citizens that are sober, charitable and attached to their homes. The peasant is good, honest, frugal and simple. When he meets a person on the highway, he invariably salutes him with " May God keep you."

Amusements are much liked by the Portuguese, who are eager after what pleases the senses. The guitar is the most popular instument of music.

They like spectacles, religious processions, bull-fights, and "arraiaes." This last means a popular reunion, something like our fairs. Dancing, music, eating, etc., constitute the principal features. Tents adorned with flags of different colors, are found in them, containing meats, fish and articles of all descriptions for sale. Some one has said, "Give to the Portuguese, arraiaes, fire-works, and few taxes, and you are sure of keeping them contented." In Portugal, bull-fights are very pleasing to even the nobility. The bulls have their horns capped with balls, thereby making this amusement less barbarous and sanguinary than in Spain, where the animals are killed with the sword, and where the horses often run round the course completely disembowelled. If the *tourada* is a very repugnant sight in Madrid, it is simply an affair of skill and strength, in Lisbon.

Horse-racing and regattas are becoming very popular in Portugal and in time these kinds of amusement will undoubtedly be presented in all their display.

The Portuguese eat more fish than meat, and there are in the markets, very many varieties of the finny tribe. Dried cod and sopa secca, a kind of soup, are very popular dishes. The red-wine of Termo is generally used to wash them down. Meat-stew, boiled-beef, pork, sausages and rice-bouillon are found, in addition to those articles mentioned above, on the tables of people in comfortable circumstances. The dinner hour is from one to two o'clock, in the country; but in the cities, it is much later.

Formerly the Portuguese travelled very little, and consquently remained in ignorance of foreign lands; but now, thanks to the facility and cheapness of communication on land as well as on sea, they are to be found in all countries. Indolent by nature, and living in one of the finest climates of the world, they are not very energetic in their occupations. The eternal *amanha* (to-morrow) is the greatest enemy of public and private well-being. Natural intelligence is a gift, which belongs to almost all the Portuguese, but true culture of mind, and a solid instruction are the portion of the minority.

In regard to morals, they differ but little at Lisbon from those of the rest of Europe. French tastes reign in that city, and in it are found all kinds of stores kept by French and Germans. Almost every one speaks French, which remains the language of the Diplomatic Corps. In society, despite that English influence, which is mentioned by all those traveling in the country, the Minister from Great Britain is often obliged to use French, as the number of Portuguese speaking English is limited, even among their statesmen, litterateurs and savants. The principal cities have their own clubs and circles, in which are to be found persons of all ranks, provided they give proof of good education. In this respect, Portugal shows herself in an advanced position, for it possesses a society in which one meets, at all times, the nobility, the clergy, the diplomatic corps, men of letters, etc.

The *grandes dames* do not always take the names of their husbands; they retain those of their families, a custom, which causes great confusion to foreigners.

Bastards enjoy a position not to be found elsewhere. At all times, legislation has favored them, whilst society receives them on the same footing as legitimate children provided they have been legally recognized. John I, the Chief of the Aviz dynasty, although a bastard, was one of the most enlightened, radiant and beloved of kings.

In regard to carriages, particularly in Lisbon, those to be hired in the streets are coupés and calèches, drawn by two horses. Private carriages are noted for a certain elegance and solidity. Many are imported from Paris or from London. The royal gala equipages deserve a special mention. They are sculptured and gilt carriages of great value, containing superb Venetian mirrors, as well as panels of a great magnificence. One of them dates from the XVIIth century. Indeed the entire collection is unique.

CONCLUDING CHAPTER ON SOCIAL LIFE.

Portuguese society is divided into the clergy, nobility, middle class and the populace.

Although the clergy have no longer the same riches and privileges as in former times, they occupy still a most eminent position, which fact can be better understood when we remember that there is a state religion, and that this religion should be an object of veneration to all. The history of the clergy is almost the history of the country, and it should receive especial attention ; but want of space requires us to forego entering upon more than a few pertinent remarks. When the monarchy was founded the clergy had as much influence as the nobility, and this influence was increased by the religious war, then carried on, with bitterness, against the infidel. The priests themselves then fought on the field of battle. They were more enlightened than the other classes ; they alone possessed the precious seeds of civilization, of which the Pope then had the initiative, and they represented in society, heaven with its sweet recompenses and its terrible punishments. It was to be expected from these circumstances, that the clergy would possess a place more important than the nobility, over whom the Church exercised an influence as efficacious as that which it exercised over the king. In fact, monasteries were founded everywhere, under the care of the monarchs and of the nobles ; very great donations in land and in privileges, placed the clergy in an extraordinary state of fortune and power, which made them stronger and bolder than the nobles and the king. The domains of the church equalled those of the state ;

the clergy possessed in them an absolute authority, and their influence starting from that, spread itself over the whole kingdom,
finding powerful auxiliaries in terrified consciences, in pious
souls, and in the general ignorance. Following the example of
the nobles, the priests meddled with all the intrigues of the
court, and often invoked the thunders of the Vatican upon
the heads of the sovereigns, who refused to comply with all
their demands. Fear often forced the monarchs to undergo the
increasing influence of the clergy, which weighed on them even
more than that of the noblity.

The expeditions sent out and the discoveries made by the
Portuguese, under the direction of the Infant D. Enrique, opened
a vast field to the ambition of the nobles, and afforded an opportunity to spread the faith. The church turned her attention to
the new fields, thus giving a moment of respite as well as some
sort of independence to the laity. The Inquisition admitted
into Portugal by the unreflecting piety, of John III., established clerical influence on a still more solid base. The results
were very pernicious to the interests of the country, to the
development of the institutions, to the progress of its civilization, and to the energy of the nation.

During the epoch of the Spanish Domination, the ecclesiastical dignitaries, leaving the illusions of patriotism to the lower
clergy, went over to the side of Phillip II., in the same manner
as the high nobility did, without troubling themselves about the
loss of Portuguese autonomy.

Although severe losses were endured afterwards, the clergy
possessed, however, up to the liberal epoch of 1834, great wealth
and many privileges. On the advent of the liberal party, D.
Pedro IV. and his ministers, put an end to such a state of
things. Perhaps they went a little too far in their desire to
make up for loss time. At the present time the clergy is poor,
and the great dignitaries of the church are no richer than the

curés. Deprived of their tithes, they remain at the charge of
the state, and are paid like other public functionaries. There is
a rate called congra, levied in each parish for the support of the
spiritual adviser. Undoubtedly the aim has been to impoverish
a class which has always shown itself opposed to liberal ideas.
The measures taken in 1834, in regard to the clergy, were marked with a severity which the events rather explain than justify ;
and when the minds of men became calm, the necessity of en-
dowing the ministers of religion in a proper manner, without
bestowing, as in the past, such vast possessions, was soon perceived.

Although the clergy may have lost some of their ancient
prestige, they exert a marked influence upon the Portuguese
people. When its members are at the same time learned and
virtuous ; more occupied with the salvation of souls than with
the wretched goods of this lower-world ; when they inspire the
consideration and respect due to their exalted mission, they are
sure of being able to count upon the devotion of faithful souls
and to direct their consciences towards the word of Christ.

The liberal reforms gave to each one his natural position, the
means of utilizing his activity, and a certain amount of legitimate inflence. The odious privileges of former times being
abolished, an end has been put to the domination of one class over
another. The nobility, under the constitutional règime, is divided into four groups ; the first includes the highest rank, hereditary or otherwise, consisting of the following : the Patriarch
of Lisbon, who precedes all, as cardinal ; dukes, marquises,
arch-bishops and counts, as well as viscounts, barons or
simple gentlemen to whom high nobility has been accorded;
bishops, peers of the kingdom, the sons and daughters of dukes
are counted amongst the first. The second group is formed by
viscounts and barons. The third is composed of the gentlemen
of the Royal Household (Fidalgos da Casa Real), and lastly the

fourth is that of the lower nobility, in which are found the chevaliers and the commanders of the military orders, the university professors, doctors in the various faculties, magistrates military officers, and ecclesiastics who have reached the sub-deaconship.

The bourgoisie is composed of those engaged in commerce, industry and the arts, as well as of agriculturists in easy circumstances. It should be remarked, however, that this class is only a transitory one between the pupulace and the nobility, thus occupying a position difficult to be found in other lands.

The orders of knighthood are the following : " Jesus Christ," "Saint Benoit d'Aviz," "Saint James of the Sword," " The Tower and the Sword," and the order of the " Conception de Villa Vicosa." The most ancient of these is that of " Christ," which is only the continuation of the " Order of the Templars "; it dates from 1318. Saint Benoit d'Aviz was created in 1162, by Alphone I.; the order of Saint James was instituted in 1177 ; the " Tower and Sword " was instituted in 1459, and was restored in 1808 ; the last order made its appearance in 1818.

At present the military commanders do not carry any pension. with them. The greatest posts, whether military or civil, are decorated with the "Order of Christ," when any great services have been rendered. The other distinctions are bestowed on various classes, according to the nature of the meritorious deed. The military and naval services receive the " Saint Benoit d'Aviz;" science, art and literature are honored with the " Saint James," whereas a brilliant feat of arms, or an act of courage, whether civil or military, will obtain for the hero the " Tower and the Sword."

These general rules have often been modified, and there does not exist, at the present time, the same exactitude or the same rigorous discrimination as in other lands. In our opinion, it is necessary either to elevate the orders or to abolish them altogether.

In concluding our remarks on the clergy, we might mention something concerning the ecclesiastical organization. The ecclesiastical division of the kingdom and the adjacent islands comprehends the patriarchate of Lisbon, the two arch-bishoprics of Braga and of Evora, and 16 bishoprics. The number of parishes was 3,788 in 1873.

The Portuguese Church forms four metropolitan provinces, of which the centres are Lisbon, Braga, Evora, and Goa for the possessions beyond the sea. Annexed is the list of the subdivisions: 1. Metropolitan province of Braga.—The Arch-bishop of Braga bears the title of "Primate of the Spains," which title is disputed with him by the arch-bishop of Toledo. The suffragan bishops are those of Porto, Braganza, Aveiro, Coimbra, Vizeu and Pinhel. 2. Metropolitan province of Lisbon.—The title of patriarch given to the prelate governing this province is simply honorary. His functions are those of an arch-bishop. His vicar-general is arch-bishop in partibus. The dignity of Cardinal is attached to that of "Patriarch of Lisbon." The suffragans are those of Lamego, Guarda, Castello Branco, Leiria and Portalegre, upon the continent; of Angra and Funchal in the adjacent islands, and of Cape Verd, St. Thomas and Angola in Africa. 3. Metropolitan province of Evora. Three bishops assist the Arch-bishop of Evora; they are those of Beja, Elvas and Faro. 4. Metropolitan province of Goa. The Arch-bishop of Goa bears the title of "Primate of the East." His suffragans are those of Cochin, Meliapor, Malacca and Timor, Macao, Nankin, Pekin, and the prelacy of Mozambique in Africa.

The arch-bishops and the other dignitaries are nominated by the king, but the nominations require to be confirmed by the Pope. The crown has the right of nomination to ecclesiastical benefices. The publication of the decrees made by councils, as well as of "letters apostolic," depends upon the authorisation or the refusal of the crown; the assent of the Chambers even is essential, when it is necessary to treat of a general question, or of the conclusion of a concordat.

The question of organizing missions beyond the sea, and of applying the best measures to present the complete ruin of the ancient "Padroado," (patronage in reference to benefices,) possessed by the Crown of Portugal, in Asia and in Africa, has recently attracted great attention.   It is as important to the Holy See as to Portugal, since it concerns the preservation of the Roman Catholic missions in Hindoostan and elsewhere, now threatened by the proselytizing societies, established in England. It might go so far as to destroy the denomination of the Portuguese in those parts.   There is a vast field in the interior of Africa, the pacification and the conquest of which, in a peaceful manner, could be effected by the Portuguese more advantageously than by any other European nation.   For, besides the fact that other nations would find it necessary to commence from the beginning, the prestige acquired from past deeds by the Portuguese is quite sufficient to allow these latter to dispense with the use of violent means.   The road has been prepared for the missionary.   He alone can effect what arms have failed to do, viz., the civilization of the subject races.

ARMY AND NAVY.

Before giving an idea of the military organization in Portugal, it would not be uninteresting to speak about the characteristic qualities of our army. Whether against the domination of the Moors, at the commencement of our history, or against the Spaniards, when these latter attempted to destroy the independence of our native land, or against the various nations in Asia and in Africa with whom we have come in contact, the Portuguese army has always given proof of a grand heroism.

This very century has seen that small nation, (undoubtedly aided by the Spanish and the English,) maintain a bold front to the victorious eagles of the "Great Napoleon." The invasion of the Peninsula by the French, was for the conquerer, a disastrous attempt. Wellington, who had been a witness on many occasions of the courage displayed by his Portuguese allies, called them "the fighting cocks of the Peninsula Army."

In regard to instruction, it must be confessed there are some improvements to be made, in order that the army may be on equal terms, in that respect, with the armies of the great central European Powers; still, it is not the less true, that much progress has been made during the past few years. The equipments are being renewed and placed in a condition suitable to the wants of the present day. As to tactics and administration, the steps advised by modern science have been adhered to, attention being paid, at the same time, to the experience acquired by the nations who are the most advanced in this subject. The country having an army which is restrained in point of size by a limited conscription, and being unable to place very considerable forces in the field, as is the case with the nations that are accustomed to drilling the entire population, it was necessary to think of organizing a good reserve. This reserve has been created, and, in case of an invasion, there would be a competent force to deal with the enemy.

The Portuguese government lately promulgated its opinion in reference to the question of ascertaining whether the action of citizens, in case of invasion, should submit to every restriction. It has been established that Portugal, not having a drilled nation behind her regular army to enter upon a campaign at the first signal, as is the case in Germany and elsewhere, it would be more than dangerous to impose any restriction on the action of her natural defenders.

Besides the reserve, a National Guard would be able to render great service in the future, if it could be mobilized without much delay.

The Portuguese army does not contain more than 30,000 men of all arms ; but this number might be diminished, if a well organized line of general defense could be counted upon. Before 1855 the system of recruiting was somewhat arbitrary, but since that date the impost of blood falls upon all classes of society, with several exceptions. Substitution is allowed, and by means of a private contract or of a sum paid to the government, which then assumes the duty of providing a substitute, a person may escape this onerous duty.

Military service is obligatory for eight years. After three years passed under the "colors," the soldier returns home, but he still belongs to the reserve, and it is only at the end of eight years that he finds himself at liberty. Usually, the number of men in active service does not exceed 20,000, the government having the power of giving furloughs to the soldiers that are not indispensable to the service. In this way there is an economy effected, and a number of hands placed at the disposal of agriculturalnecessities. There are military five divisions, of which the centresare, Lisbon, Vizen, Porto, Evora and Angra.

The Portuguese army, in time of peace, is on the following basis:

Officers of general staff,	··········	32
" Corps "	··········	31
" Engineers,	··········	58
" Artillery,	··········	198
" Cavalry,	··········	224
" Infantry,	··········	930
	Total officers,	1,473

Rank and file:

Engineers,	508
Artillery,	3,012
Cavalry,	3,184
Infantry,	23,316
Total officers and men,	31,493

In time of war the numbers could be raised to 70,000.

The cannon-foundry, annexed to the general depot of war-material is abundantly supplied with all the recent appurtenances designed to perfect the manufacture of canon, and from it have issued almost all rifled guns as well as mitrailleuses, employed in the Portuguese army. Here have been made the various necessaries, so essential to a force desiring to be ready to enter upon the performance of its duties at any moment.

We cannot enter into any further details. But sufficient has been said to make it apparent that a corps d'armée of at least 50,000 men could be placed in line of battle. To the well-known bravery of the Portuguese soldiers, it will be necessary henceforward to add a rigorous discipline, which our unhappy civil wars have enfeebled to a certain extent. An army of brave men, well disciplined, well instructed and well equipped, will be

able, in case of emergency, to preserve intact the national honor
and independence, especially since its role will always be de-
fensive and never aggressive.

If we compare the Portuguese navy with what it was in former times, we shall find it to be but a shadow ; but if we consider what it was a few years ago, our surprise will be excited
at the great improvement that has taken place. The navy is
now more in accordance with the colonial needs. The aim has
been to make it sufficiently large so that our flag might be respected in our distant possessions, at the same time that the
means of a communication with them are rendered easier. The
ministers of the navy for the past few years have applied themselves with zeal to the restoration of our naval glory, and we see
with satisfaction that already the effective force is in a state to
supply the most urgent wants of the service.

The complete transformation will require some time yet,
since the Portuguese government, adopting the same policy as it
follows in regard to the army and the military fortifications,
limits itself to such results as can be conveniently obtained, in
the present state of the treasury.

The ships, the equipment of which was proposed for 1873–
1874, are as follows :

Ships.	Officers and Crew.	Guns.
6 Steam Corvettes,···················1,286		78
4 Steam Gun-boats, ····················	309	13
2 Screw Steamers,····················	150	4
1 Side-wheel Steamer,··· ···············	127	7
1 Steam Transport, ···················	90	
8 Sailing-vessels,····················	461	48

Ships Out of Commission.	Guns.
2 Steam Corvettes, ·······························	32
4 Steam Gun-boats,·······························	14
6 Sailing-vessels, ·······························	135

There are besides a few vessels of small dimensions, which
are used in the colonies.

There are 9 vessels being constructed in England; 1 transport of 1,500 tons, and of a horse power of 1,250; 2 corvettes, 1,000 tons and 900 h. p. each; three gun-boats, each of 530 tons and of 500 h. p; two river gun-boats of 280 tons and 40 h. p. each, and finally, an ironclad (broadside) of 1,500 tons and 3,200 h. p. These vessels, the cost of whose armaments will amount to about 1,750 contos, are intended to replace those that are obsolete.

Ever since 1862, the number of the armed ships allowed of a naval resolve at Lisbon. It has been a practical school, of which our marine had, prior to that period, stood in great need. There is now a special school to train sailors, on board a vessel moored in the Tagus. The effects of the improvements introduced have been beneficial. The skillful manœuvering of the Portuguese fleet has elicited the admiration of foreign spectators.

There is no corps of marine infantry or artillery. The corps of marines performs on board ship, the duties of gunners, and of the seamen. That organization has produced very good results. The corps is divided into three divisions and is composed of nearly 2,000 men.

Annexed is the table of the Naval Heirarchy :

Vice-Admiral,	1
Rear-Admirals,	4
Post Captains,	8
Captains of Frigates,	18
Commanders,	24
First Lieutenants,	48
Second Lieutenants,	90

There are, in addition, about 233 officers and personages of various ranks, such as chaplains, naval constructors, doctors, paymasters, pursers, etc.

The Supreme Council of Military Justice takes cognizance of the crimes and faults committed by the individuals belonging to the naval forces. The merchant marine is, in some cases, subject to the same tribunal. (6)

The Marine Hospital in Lisbon is an excellent establishment of its kind; we should mention also the Marine Barracks. As regards the material for the fleet, there are two principal depots, the Marine Arsenal and the National Rope-yard, both of which are in Lisbon. The Arsenal is a vast edifice, containing the construction yards, depots of arms, munitions and provisions, the Naval Museum and School. Although the arsenal has produced very fine vessels, we find ourselves compelled, like many other nations, to have recourse to the ship-yards of England, when we wish to have men-of-war without delay, and at a lower rate. Probably we do not yet possess suitable machines, etc., in our yards. It would not be amiss to refer to the recent purchase of a transport in the United States.

The rope-walk situated in Lisbon, on the banks of the Tagus, employs 200 workmen. There are made all the ropes, cables and sails, destined for the navy. This establishment, being in possession of the best mechanical means, rivals similar ones in other lands.

For purposes of marine conscription, the coast is divided into four departments ruled by "intendants," and each department into seventeen maritime districts.

An advance has been made. In a not very remote future, we shall possess a navy on a scale adequate to our wants as a colonial nation. Not being designed to take the offensive, it will prove sufficent for all the purposes we may have in regard to the maintainance of our national autonomy and the preservation of our colonial empire.

EDUCATION.

Some years ago, instruction in Portugal was in a very imper-
fect condition ; the number of primary schools was deplorably
deficient ; the methods of teaching, unpractical, and the
teachers badly paid. As regards secondary education, which
corresponds with that obtained in academies in this country,
great defects have always existed. Latin, the elementary principles of mental and moral Philosophy, Rhetoric, Algebra and
Geometry, were studied with some degree of success; but History
and Geography were very much neglected. The want of knowledge in the last two branches, had a bad effect upon the future
of such students as were admitted to the superior courses in the
University. The study of the science in general was very superficial, because of the want of a good and solid foundation. In
the University of Coimbra, the greatest attention was paid to
Law and to Theology. The doctrines however were superannuated, and the professors were unfortunately attached to a
defective routine. The departments of Philosophy, Mathematics
and Medicine were exceptions to this rule. Whilst the positive
sciences remained stationary, the natural sciences followed, more
or less, the paths trodden abroad. This state of things was not
very encouraging. But to-day, although there is much to be
done in regard to public education, it must be confessed that our
system of instruction is a thousand times better than it was formerly. Primary instruction is extending itself throughout the
kingdom, and the creation of schools for the two sexes attracts
the daily attention of the Portuguese Official Gazette. The methods
have been improved, and the school-masters, without being

well paid, have less reason to complain. Very good elementary
text-books have been introduced for the use of the educational
institutions. As to geographical studies, it must be declared
that there is much to be done in Portugal. It is a singular
circumstance that the nation so celebrated in the past for its
geographical discoveries, has shown itself indifferent, of late, to
this subject. However, Portugal lately made a respectable display at the International Geographical Exhibition in Paris, and
it is to be hoped that some great steps in advance will soon be
made.

At Coimbra there are five faculties, Law, Theology, Philosophy, Mathematics and Medicine. The present educational
organization depends almost entirely upon a decree of the 20th
of December, 1844, which contains some salutary dispositions.
But it is reasonable to suppose that, in the course of thirty-two
years, a re-organization has become indispensable. A reform
proposed by the present "Minister of the Interior," Rodrigues
Sampayo, is to be discussed in the Chambers. The department
of public instruction is under the jurisdiction of that minister.
A consulting committee is in immediate charge. All the duties
of administration etc., are attended to by it in the same manner
as by the "Boards of Education" in other lands.

By the proposed reform, it is enacted that all children from
6 to 12 years of age, with the usual exceptions, must attend some
place of instruction, whether public or private. Attention is paid
to the number of times the pupils are present. The aim has been
to make the districts capable of managing their own schools, instead of depending upon the central government. The latter
always pays a certain quota of the cost incurred in erecting the
necessary edifices, etc. The desire is to form what, in this country, are called district committees, and to leave in their hands all
the details naturally connected with the schools. The government will then vote annually a certain sum, which will be suffi-

cient to assist the parish or district committee in an efficient manner.

Thanks to the energetic steps already taken, great success has been achieved. Whereas the number of primary schools had increased from 455 in 1772, to only 991 in 1838, the increase has been more rapid during the last quarter of the century, as can be seen by the following figures :

1854 ···1,189
1865 ···.2,123
1870 ···.2,359

The regular scholars numbered 52,720 boys, and 10,217 girls, in 1869. Of course there is a large number educated in private schools, etc. It was ascertained that in 1864, there were 22,970, in such establishments. Since that date, the number has undoubtedly increased to a great extent.

This public education is divided into two classes; primary and secondary. The former consists of reading, writing, the elements of arithmetic, geography, history, grammar, deportment, and christian doctrine : in the latter we meet with an advanced stage of the same studies as in the primary. Geometry as applied to industry, and linear drawing, are also taught. Other subjects are introduced, according to the proficiency of the class.

There is one circumstance that militates against the rapid advance of primary education in Portugal. It is the want of good teachers. The salaries are so low that the profession does not afford many inducements to young persons to engage in it. This objection would have been long ago removed, had it not been for the impoverishment of the public treasury.

Normal schools have been established in Lisbon, Porto, Coimbra, Evora, and in Vizeu, so that some assistance is offered thereby to the training of teachers for their important mission.

Secondary education is in a more advanced stage. Yet it requires some reforms. By the decree of 1844, a lyceum was es-

tablished in the chef-lieu of each district. Besides these lyceums, there are schools of equal rank supported by the government. The general course of studies extends over five years, and
embraces Portuguese, Latin, the Humanities, History, Elementary
Mathematics, Elements of Physics, Chemistry and of Natural History; the principles of Natural Law, Literature, Rhetoric, Linear
Drawing, French and English. Greek is taught in the schools
of the first grade, and Hebrew at Santarem, Coimbra, and Lisbon. In the last city there is a chair of Arabic. German is
taught at Porto, Coimbra, and Lisbon.

The number of pupils in the lyceum was

in 1867—1868··············3,121
"   1868—1869··············2,912
"   1869—1870··············3,126

In the official schools of the same rank, there were 704 students, in 1864; but this number fell to 618 in the following
year.

Portugal possesses, as establishments of superior instruction,
the University of Coimbra, the Polytechnic school of Lisbon,
the Polytechnic Academy of Porto, the schools of Medicine and
of Surgery in Lisbon, Porto and Funchal, and the superior
course in literature.

There are, moreover, the Military College, Army School, Naval School, the Royal Conservatory of Lisbon, and many others.
But we have not the space to enter into an account of these, especially since they are analogous to those existing in other
countries.

Agriculture. Industry and Finances.

In a work on the rural economy of Portugal, published five years ago, we find some note-worthy remarks. According to M. Rebeleo daSilva, the Kingdom of Portugal is divided into four agricultural districts of unequal extent; the north, the centre, the south and the mountains. M. Leince de Lavergne be lieves, however, that it would be simpler to admit of only three regions, each containing 3,000,000 hectares; the first, which might be termed the maritime, or western, bordering along the coast, comprising the ancient province of Minho, one of the richest and best cultivated countries in Europe, the half of da Beira, and a great portion of Estremadura, is, without doubt, the most prosperous. The second, or the mountainous region, composed of Tras-os-montes, the remainder of da Beira and of Estremadura, is studded with mountains. The third, or the southern, comprising Alemtejo, and the little Kingdom of Algarves, is justly considered the least cultivated.

According to a memorial addressed to the Minister of Agriculture in 1868, half of the 9,000,000 hectares remains uncultivated. It is in the coast districts that we find the land treated in a comparatively scientific manner. · The agricultural production of Portugal is chiefly composed of cereals ; indian corn, wheat, buck-wheat, barley, oats and rice being the principal constituents. But the amount raised is insufficient for internal consumption. The vegetables, as arranged according to their importance, are potatoes, French beans, chick-peas, vetches, lussines, ordinary peas and lentels.

The country produces oranges, lemons, figs, almonds, as well as the fruits that are found in the orchards of Northern Europe. The olive trees produce a large quantity of oil, the preparation of which is being improved every day. The production of hemp and flax, does not suffice for home use. To these articles we should add cork, besides the products of the adjacent isles, such as coffee, sugar, tobacco and cotton, although these last are cultivated to a very small extent.

There are forests in Estremadura and the provinces of the North, which if treated in a suitable manner, would well repay all the necessary outlay, especially at this time when the means of transportation are becoming numerous. The various kinds of wood, as well as large quantities of turpentine, are the products of these forests. The pines of the forest of Leiria, and the celebrated forest of Bussaco, not far from Coimbra, with its magnificent Lebanon Cedars and Indian Cypresses, are very remarkable. The delicious hills of Cintra, covered with orange and lemon groves, appear destined to maintain alive forever the mythological tradition of the garden of the Hesperides. M. de Lavergne thinks perhaps with reason, that the future of the country depends principally upon its aboriculture. In this respect there remains much to do.

The olive tree as well as the mulberry and other fruit bearing trees, occupy the first rank in the aborisation of Portugal. The olive gives only a mediocre return and extends over only 42,000 hectares of ground. France alone buys from us oil to the value of 25,000,000 francs annually. The culture of silk-worms is increasing with the development of mulberries. The return from the silk-worms in 1868 reached 2,000,000 kilogrammes, of a value of 8,400,000 francs. England and France were our principal customers in that article. Portugal was fortunate in escaping the disease which caused so much distruction among the worms in the other parts of Europe.

The country formerly produced scarcely enough wine for internal consumption. There is a doubt whether any wine was exported, as some chronicles state, before the reign of Ferdinand I, in the 14th century. But it is certain that, at the epoch of our glorious discoveries, galleons sailed for the Indies, supplied with our wines. This fact proves that even then the great lasting power of the Portuguese wines was known. During a period of great sterility in Italy, English merchants came for the first time to seek the black wines then produced on the banks of the Douro, near Lamego. The English houses in Oporto bought wines there and sent them to the English markets. There existed then an exportation of wines from Oporto and Lisbon, to the Baltic, to Brazil and elsewhere. But the greater part was taken up by England. From 1678 to 1702, that amount did not exceed 5,612 pipes annually. The yearly average of Oporto wines exported to England from 1703 to 1756, was not over 16,218 pipes; from 1789 to 1815, it rose to 42,000 pipes. After the Napoleonic wars, this increase disappeared, and we find the average from 1815 to 1834, to be only 23,000 pipes. This was owing to the establishment by England of equal custom dues on all wines.

By means of careful analysis, oenologists have ascertained that, despite their great deversity, Portuguese wines are wholly without adulteration, on which account, they are appetizing, salubrious and lasting. It is a fact that, from our different grapes, all the wines known in the markets of the world can be made, without altering their natural condition. All that is necessary is to adopt such methods as have been recommended by certain oenologists, among whom we find Vicomte de Villa Maior, Ferreira Lapa, Antonio Auguste d'Aguiar, R. de Moraes Soares, and the enlightened Minister of Andrade Corvo, who as Minister of Public Works in 1866 and 1867, took the initiative steps.

The internal consumption absorbs six-sevenths of the production; the rest is exported. It is not known out of Portugal that we have an uncultivated space of 1,000,000 hectares, all of which are admirably adapted for vineyards. Leaving aside the other localities, and speaking of only the two river districts along the Tagus, there could be raised within five or six years, millions of hectolitres of excellent wines, in addition to what is now produced. As the cultivation of these lands promises to be a very profitable investment, several projects are on foot to utilize them. Men of capital were attracted by the very favorable appearances of the wines displayed by Portugal at the last Exposition in London. Should these projects be successful, wines will be supplied to the markets of the world, at a much lower rate than at present; thus affording to persons of moderate means, the opportunity of substituting a nutritious wine for the adulterated stuff which they now purchase at an exorbitant rate. Eminent personages, such as Count de Casal Ribeiro, Antonio Augusto d'Aguiar, Anselmo Braumcamp, Palha de Faria Lacerda and José de Mello Gouvea, are devoting their attention to this important subject. We may expect some results very soon.

For the past five years the average annual production has not been less than 3,700,000 hectolitres. That production is annually distributed in the following manner:

Internal consumption at the rate of 70 litres   Hectolitres.
to each person,............. 2,800,000
Exportation,................................... 369,388
Distillation, Vinegar, etc., ... 550,612
Total 3,720,000

The exportation for the past five years ending in 1873:

	Quantity (Hectolitres).	Value (Reis)
1869	325,353	6,904,393,300
1870	340,501	9,655,676,000
1871	341,484	7,742,655,000
1872	402,145	9,125,343,140
1873	437,459	9,689,183,759
Average	369 388	8 423,450,239

Portugal was represented in the last wine exposition in London in order that the knowledge of our ordinary wines might be extended. These wines are cheaper, more varied, and less charged with alchohol than Port and Madeira. The Commissioner from Portugal was desirous of discussing the question concerning the fictitious Port and other wines, which innundated the English market, and also of inquiring into the real state of all matters connected with the sale of Portuguese wines in England.

England has not consented until now to the request made by her own Chambers of Commerce as well as by the Portugese Government, to modify and to a certain extent, to diminish the high custom dues levied on Portugese wines. Owing to natural strength, our wines are compelled to pay really 150 °/₀ more than French wines, although the tax, based on an alcoholic scale, is the same for all. Despite the indisposition of the British Government to accede to our proposition, we do not find that the importation of the Douro wines has lessened. The importation into England of those wines advanced from 35,619 pipes in 1864, to 56,531 pipes in 1874. When the area for exportation increases, we may be sure that the area of production will be extended over the 1,000,000 hectares which have not yet been cultivated.

Although the pasturage is good, the rearing of cattle meets with serious difficulties by reason of excessive drouths and the want of artificial meadows. The beef cattle, the most considerable in numbers, are not fully developed. The horses, destitute of fine forms, are vigorous. Birds, poultry and game abound. We find hares, boars, partridges, deer, wild ducks, quails, and many other kinds of game. Among the productions which belong to the animal and the vegitable kingdoms, we could mention the cochineal, which could, like silk, become an important resource for the Azores.

Agricultural industry in Portugal is followed in four different systems: actual culture by the proprietor himself, farm renting

on shares, and by long leases. Small holdings are the rule, but
farming on a large scale also exists, and promises to be developed
still more. Agricultural machines are being successfully introduced into the country. Their introduction will, undoubtedly,
improve the present system. An agricultural work lately written
by Sr. Andrade Corvo, will, henceforth, be of great utility for
Portuguese farmers. Had we space we should do more than
advert to it.

In conclusion, let us take a general glance at Portuguese agriculture, whilst citing the words of M. de Laveignier in his study
on the rural economy of Portugal. "Portugal is, by proportion,
richer and more thickly inhabited than Spain, Corsica, Sardinia,
Greece and all the analogeous countries. Portugal might be
compared with the sixteen departments which form the Provin-
çal region of France. Those departments measure 9,000,000
hectares, the exact extent of Portugal. The climate is not different
and the productions are the same. Mr. Perry in a recent publication, calculates the urban population of the kingdom at 706-
500 individuals, and the rural at 3,583,500. The latter, therefore, bear a proportion to the whole population of five to six.
As Portugal is an agricultural country, its territory should suffice for the maintenance of at least twice her present population.
The average production of the cereals mentioned in the beginning of this article reaches 890,615,000 kilogrammes. The
average importation of foreign wheat, flour, corn and rye, is
40,969,986 kilogrammes. The average importation of wheat
from the Azores is 5,664,110 moios. It may seem strange that
there is a necessity for importing food. But this seeming anam-
aly is due to the fact that the agricultural efforts of Portugal are
not by any means energetic. However, a smiling and prosperous
future is before them if the Portuguese will but devote themselves to that occupation, which is the production of all national
wealth, agriculture.

Other countries less fortunate in their soil and climate, such as Bulgium and Holland, afford shining examples of what can be effected by industry combined with frugality, even when nature is apparently hostile. Nature being on the contrary, very beneficent in her gifts to the Portuguese, it remains for them to acquire wealth and happiness, by means of active and persevering labor. All the elements of success are present. Let it be their care to apply them in an indefatigable manner.

Portugal is rather agricultural than industrial. There are, however, some industries pursued with success, the most important being the mineral. Some years ago, hardly any attention was paid to mining in that country, so much had that branch of public wealth been neglected. Only some savants reflected on the great role which, in a future more or less distant, it would play. The mineral production, a dozen years ago, was confined to a coal mine at S. Pedro da Cova and Buarcos. The S. Domingos mine has since offered new horizons to this industry, and the importance of its development has been fully recognized. It is, of its kind, the most considerable in the Penisula. The explorations made in other parts of the country, and the great number of the concessions demanded and obtained, give to the question a great importance. Minerals are, then, a recent article of export. Leaving aside the exportation from the S. Domingos mine, from which are extracted more than 200,000 tons annually which are embarked at a contiguous port. In 1873, there left the Tagus, 22,091 tons of iron, 4,039 of copper, 6,125 of manganese and 2,267 of phosphate, making a total of 35,022 tons. The iron is derived from the mines of Monges and of Serrinha, the working of which has only just commenced. Iron is met with in other districts, as has been ascertained from recent explorations. On the 31st of December, 1872, there were 250 mines conceded, whether provisionally or definitively, of which eighty-eight were in active working. Thirty-one of them contained manganese, sixteen copper, fifteen lead and silver, nine iron, nine tin, five coal, twenty-eight antimony and one bitumen.

The considerable gains realized by foreigners who took hold of the mines, have at last attracted the attention of the Portuguese public, and the capitalists of the country are engaged in the work of opening mines in various districts. The Transtagana Mining Company possess four mines at Agustrel, which are rich in copper. As the metal is found in masses, rather than in veins, there is a scientific presumption that there is in these mines an almost inexhaustible quantity.

Portugal is very rich in marbles, lime-stones and free-stones. It would be tedious, however, to enter into any details regarding them.

As to manufacturing industry, we can mention wool, silk and linen as being worthy of special attention. The province of Beira presents the woolen industry in its greatest development, and it is the City of Covilha, which occupies the first rank in this manufacture. The factories of that locality, produce casimeres, velvet, cloths, raglans, saragossas, linsly-woolseys, shawls and other articles. These factories annually consume 1,500,000 kilogrammes of wool. Lisbon and Oporto furnish them the chemicals and drugs, and Spain sends indigo and large quantities of cochineal and madder. The sumac comes from Villa Nova de Foz Coa, the pastel from the district of Guardo, and the soap from the Spanish frontiers. Brazil and the Portuguese colonies, are the principal outlets for the products of this national industry. The silk manufacture is very ancient in Portugal, where it has had great privileges. Under the Marquis de Pombal, a model for spinning manufactory was established near Braganza, at the expense of the state, and the silks obtained thence rivaled those of Italy. Advancing step by step, the Portuguese silks were preferred to those of England. Although they have now fallen back a little, owing to their inability to contend with the French and the English establishments, Portuguese factories continue to produce excellent velvets, ribbons, laces, etc. The silks are prepared at Lisbon, Lamego, Porto, Sinfaes, Amarante, Marco de Canavezes, Povoa de Lanhoso, Armamar, Valenco and Funchal. The principal markets are the Portuguese colonies in Asia and in Africa, Brazil and Spain.

This industry will play an important part in our commerce of the future, if the artisans and others engaged in it will adopt the designs and colors introduced into silk manufacture by the French and the English.

.The manipulation of flax–seed is very considerable at Lisbon, Oporto, Coimbra, Aviro, Santaremn, Guimarães and other localities. The principle products from it are sewing thread, linens of all kinds, table linen, laces, curtains etc.

The musiin manufactured at Guimaraes rivals that of foreign lands. Portuguese laces deserve a special mention. They are the result of an industry of modest proportions, exercised exclusively by the women at Vianna de Minho, Horta, Island of Fayal, Peniche, Setubal, and Villa do Conde. They are of the Honiton kind, closely imitating guipure and chantilly, but they are all made with the spindle. Its annual value mounts up to 30,000,000 reis. As soon as they become better known in England and the United States the demand will become very great, as they are of a really excellent character. Hitherto Spain and Brazil have been the only markets for this industry.

The manufacture of hats and of shoes exists on a great scale, in order to supply the demands made by the country, Brazil and Spain. The superior kind of shoes made in Lisbon quite equal the best Parisian. The expositions at London and Paris acknowledged the skill of the Portuguese shoe–makers.

Metallurgy commences to reach importance in Lisbon and in Oporto. In both cities are to be found well equipped foun-

dries and machine shops for steam engines and agricultural machines. Chemical products, objects of wicker work and cane,
tanned leather, cables, ropes, watches, cutlery, and finally furni-
ture, are produced. The ceramic art is very far advanced. The
manufactory of Marinha Grande, near Leiria, for glasses and
crystals, and those of Vista Alegre at Aveiro, and of Sacavene in
the Lisbon District, for porcelain, are good. Printing has made
great progress in Portugal; it is the industry, perhaps, that has
made the greatest progress. Two causes, however, militate
against the future of printing. These causes are the duties laid
on foreign paper, and the small demand for works of any kind.

There is an association in Lisbon for the encouragement of
manufacturing industries. Of this association, the King is the
protector. That personage displays the greatest interest in all
the proceedings of the society. The aim has been to get up industrial expositions to improve the methods of manufacture and
to instruct the working classes, by establishing libraries and reading rooms. The illustrious Marquis d'Avila et de Bolama, whose
name is joined to all useful enterprises, is the president.

The value of the principal articles exported rise from 898,-
582,000 reis, in 1851, to 1,431,803,700 reis in 1861.

At the Vienna Exposition there were 430 out of 878 exhibitors, rewarded. The necessity of organizing industrial statistics
and of having a journal which shall devote itself exclusively to
arts and trades, is felt every day. In Portugal there are want-
ing elementary books for the instruction of the industrial class;
but we can hope that such a deficiency will not last long. A
good technological dictionary should be supplied at once. The
prix d'honneur was accorded by the Vienna Jury to the Museum of the Portuguese Colonies, the collections of which displayed
the chief materials for the most important industries in the world.
In the second group, "Agriculture, Horticulture, and Forest
Industries," we find 312 Portuguese exhibitors, of whom 108

were recompensed; in the fourth, "Alimentary Substances, beverages included," there were 322 exhibitors, of whom 110 obtained rewards; in the fifth, " Industries (textiles), etc.," we have 120 exhibitors and 89 prizes, and in the third, " Chemical Arts," 45 exhibitors and 33 prizes.

We should at this point render homage to the memory of the late Fradesso da Selveira who was the Royal Commissioner at Vienna. He contributed the most to the remarkably successful appearance our different industries presented in that Exposition; and no little of the success our exhibitors met with is to be attributed to the indefatigable efforts made by him.

The principal articles of export, are wines, vegetables, fruits, olive oil, palm oil, minerals and marbles, skins, leather, ivory, dried meat, wool, salt, fish, colonial products, shoes, ropes, silks, etc.

Our chief markets for exportation and importation are, Great Britain, Brazil, Spain, France, and the African colonies. The value of the importations rise from 25,341,000,000 reis in 1870 to 27,164,000,000 reis in 1871 to 29,124,000,000 reis in 1872, and to 32,414,000,000 reis in 1873. The exports amount to 20,293,000,000 reis in 1870, to 21,461,000,000 in 1871, to 23,240,000,000 in 1872, and 23,291,000,000 in 1873.

If it is observed that the values mentioned in the official documents are aproximate for the great majority of goods, and defective for the exports, by taking into consideration the discrepancy between the values as ascertained from England and from France, we can conclude that we are not very far from an equilibrium in the exports and imports.

The following table is instructive :

Value of coined gold imported into Portugal.
    1870 ··,1,140 centos
    1871 ··3,591   "
    1872 ··1,795   "
    1873 ··3 917   "

The exports of specie have been insignificant during the same period.   (7)

The customs were 3,677, centos in 1860, or 50,000,000 francs; to-day they exceed 50 000,000 francs annually. In a vast country like the United States, all these figures might appear very modest, speaking absolutely, but they do not the less denote the great progress our country has made although small in territory. The State, not having since 1872, contracted a foreign loan besides the one placed on the market by the house of Erlanger in London, (the amount of which loan being nearly equal to that of the floating foreign debt paid at the same time) the importation of specie mentioned above can have but a flattering signification in regard to the financial condition of the country. What gives more importance to this fact is that, during the years previous to 1872, despite the considerable loans contracted in London the exportation of specie exceeded the importation. Now the sending abroad of gold takes place only for the purpose of paying the coupons on the foreign debt, which occurs every six months in London, Paris and Amsterdam.

The navigation has also followed a progressive scale. Several reasons could be mentioned. But undoubtedly the development of the commerce between Europe and South America through Lisbon has had the greatest influence. The number of steamships entering the Tagus is very considerable. In 1865, there were 378,494 tons of merchandise imported, and 187,156 tons exported, with 11,612 re-exported, making a grand total of 577,262 tons. In 1874 the exportations and importations amounted to 966,431 tons, making an increase of 389,169 tons. In 1869, 731 steamships, measuring 574,356 tons, and 1,787 sailing vessels, of 229,384 tons, entered the port of Lisbon; in 1873, there were 1,109 steamers of 784,819 tons, and 2,196 ships of 289,236 tons. In 1874, there entered 1,259 steamers and 2,266 ships.

The progress of the exportation by Lisbon represented in tons
offers us the following results:

1870··································35,000 tons.
1871··································44,000 "
, 1872··································49,000 "
1873··································69,000 "

There also the ports of Oporto, Figueira, Setubal, Vianna,
Caminha, Sines, etc., in which the progress has been similar.
One exception exists, viz: Vianna do Minho, where the trade has
declined in favor of Oporto, owing to the new routes of communication opened through Minho. It would be a great step in
advance, if attention were paid to the indispensable works for
improving the mouths of the ports by removing the bars. A
complete system of light houses should be established. The want
of them has been seriously felt. We might profit by the excellent
works on light houses, prepared by the learned Professor Henry
of the Smithsonian Institute. The docks in the islands of S.
Michel and Fayal, two of the Azores, will render great service
to the navigation which is growing up so rapidly between the
two worlds. By the decree of January 1st, 1875, the quarantine
organization was placed on a footing more harmonious with the
necessities of free navigation, taking charge of the public health
at the same time.

The railroads have also followed the movement forward, as
the following figures prove: in 1868, the receipts were 1,019
contos, and in 1873, 1,713 contos. The length of the secondary
lines is constantly growing, thus affording a new element to the
circulation.

In October, 1873, the length of the railroads in operation was
795 kilometres (about 500 miles) without counting 80 kilometres
of tram way. There are besides 74 kilometres in construction.
The subsidies granted by the government to the different companies for the construction of the Northern and State railroads,
were 12,786,604 milreis for the Southern, and for the South-

eastern, 3,821,793: a total of 16,608,397 milreis. Besides this sum, the company of the south-eastern railroad has received 8,325,000 milreis or $7,250,000.

The revenues derived from the post-office and the telegraphs, which amounted to only 493 contos in 1868–69, were 676 contos in 1872–73.

We have, more than once, made allusion to our financial situation, we shall now give the figures themselves. If we compare the fiscal receipts of the country in the budget of 1850–51, with those of 1874–75, we find a very satisfactory result. The receipts for 1850–51 were only 10,260 contos, whereas for the last year, they amounted to 22,304 contos. They have therefore more than doubled. This advance in the budget receipts coincides with an increasing amelioration in the effective receipt of the public revenues, which amounted to 22.234 contos in 1872–73. Thus the deficit, so common in former years, has therefore disappeard. On that desire was founded the success of a large credit operation. which the government lately undertook for the purpose of buying up the large floating debt, the heavy charges of which weighed upon the treasury. The most remarkable and significant fact in connection with our financial condition, is to be found in the realization in the country itself, without having recourse to foreign assistance of a loan of 38 000 contos, taken up by national capitalists. It was believed abroad that the country would not be able to disembarrass itself so soon. of its implacable creditors. Hereafter we shall be able to depend upcn our own capitalists, instead of being compelled to resort to the money markets of other lands.

Let us now see how our resources have been accumulated in so short a period. Since 1851, the public debt has been the culminary point of attraction for the available capital of the country. According to the report of the financial interest in

1851-52 the principal of the debt without counting fractions, was as follows:

30th of June, 1852, Internal debt,............34 904 contos.
"   "   " External debt,............42,902   "

Total, ...77 806 contos.

In the budget presented to the Cortes for 1874–75, there was demanded for the purpose of settling the interest, the sum of 10 570 contos, which at 3%, would make the principal 352 333 contos. But in this interest are included 442 contos, for the interest of bonds in the possession of the treasury. 14 739 contos should therefore be subtracted from the nominal debt, which would then be reduced to 337,594 contos. The interest payment is divided in the following manner.*

Interest for the foreign debt,.................4 194 contos.
"   "   " internal "   ....5 934   "

According to these figures the nominal debt is found to be 139 794 contos for the external, and 197 800 for the internal. The subjoined table might be instructive.

1851—1852.	Contos.
External debt,..................................	42,902
Internal "	34 904
1874—1875.	**C. ntos.**
External debt,..................................	139.794
Internal "	199,800

There has been, therefore, an increase of 96,092 contos in the external, and an increase of 162 896 in the internal. This last sum reduced to one half, that is to say at the rate of 6° ₀ which is the normal rate of the money market, represents an effective capital of 81 000 contos, as having been placed by the country in the internal public debt since 1851. We should, however, observe, when speaking of this mass of "richesse mobiliére," that the external debt is also owned, to a great extent, in Portugal, although, on account of the want of precise information,

*Subtracting the interest on the bonds possessed by the treasury.

we do not know the total.   However the "Committee of Public Credit," to which are allowed the necessary funds to pay the debt interest, paid in Lisbon, during the first six months of 1874, coupons on the external debt to the amount of 112 contos, which would represent a capital of 9,811 contos as held in Portugal.

The Spanish *rentes* in the treasury are valued at from 12,000 to 15,000 contos.   Portugal possesses very large sums in Brazilian bonds, as well as in those of other countries.   On account of the absence of official statements relative to this matter, the amount cannot be approximated..   Besides state bonds, there is a security in Portugal, which like the first, has the guarantee of the state, and which the government will soon make use of to defray the expenses of constructing the railroads of Minho and Douro. The obligations sent forth (to the value of 1,500 contos) for this purpose have augmented the "richesse mobiliere," and if the figures are not important, they possess a certain significance, when we consider the special nature of the security, and the end towards which tends the capital brought to light by that oper. ation.

Lately when the government opened the books for a subscription of 1,755 contos of the second series of obligations for the same railways, 82,000 contos were offered.

The Lisbon Chamber of Commerce estimates 50,000 contos as representing the amount consecrated by the country to its industrial and its commercial activity, through anonymous societies, credit establishments, insurance companies, factories, etc.

In the course of the financial year 1873–74, there were formed twenty-eight companies under the limited liability system, with an initial capital of 11,521 contos.   The General Society of Agricultural Credit figures for 2,160 contos; different credit establishments constituted at Oporto, and in the provinces for 6,990 contos, and mining and other companies for about 2,360 contos.

In the Budget for 1874–75 the receipts from all sources were calculated at 23,151,432,000 reis; the expenses at 24,129,133,595 reis.   There is therefore a deficit of 976,701,595 reis; but this deficit disappears for two reasons; firstly, we have placed the ordinary and the extraordinary expenses together; secondly, the sum representing the deficit will disappear soon, because of the anticipated progressive increase of the estimated public revenues. It might be said that we employ nearly half of our income to pay the iuterests on the various debts; but these debts have served to develope the productive force of the country, thereby bringing about our present relative prosperity.

It is to be wished that, in the near future, we shall devote an annual sum to the erasing of the debt-principal, as was decreed in 1845.

In the general charges we include:

	Reis.
The civil list for the Royal Family,···············	592,000 000
Expenses of the Cortes,····························	84,731,892
Interest and the debt charges,····················	644 078,000
Different charges and inactive classes,·············	572 838 088
Total,·····························1,893,647,980	

The expenses of the Ministries:

	Reis.
Finance,·······································	1 561,004 085
Interior, ·····································	1 928 579,515
Justice and clergy,····························	519,655 987
War,··	3,422,180,094
Marine, ······································	1,224 000,426
Foreign Affairs,·······························	252 230,254
Public Works, Commerce and Industry,········	1,321,514,617
Total,·····························10,229,164,978	

Extraordinary Expenses.

R-is.

Ministry of Justice, subsidies to religious, etc.,····	2.4C0 C00
To the Minister of Marine, for repairs, etc.,······	45 0C0 0C0
Public works,···································1,020,0C0 000
Surveys and preservation of railroads,············	368.480,000

Total,································1,435,8b0,000

The receipts are derived from the following source.

Direct Taxes,·····································	5,645,220,C00
Postage and Registration, ·····················	2,598,2(0,CC0
Indirect Taxes, ·······························	11,831,330,CC0
National property and various other revenues,··	2,633,966.CC0
Interest on bonds in Treasury,··················	433,716,0C0

23,152,432,000

The ordinary expenses.

General charges,································	1,893,647.980
Interest on debt,·······························	10,570,440,637
The expenses for the various ministries,·······	10,229,164,978

Total,······ 22,693,253,595

Extraordinary Expenses,····················· 1,435,880,000

24,129,133,595

THE COLONIES.

Portugal possesses, even now, excellent Colonies, the reliques of her once rich patrimony. In the historical sketch we spoke about the famous discoveries of the Portuguese, and of the glorious traditions which our ancestors left us. Our task now is to show the present state of those colonies, and the prosperity which they have acquired during the past few years, thereby accompanying the civilizing development of the mother-country. '

Our posessions beyond the sea, containing an area of 45,842 square leagues, are composed of six provinces, viz: Cape Verd Islands; St. Thomas and Prince; Angola, Ambriz and Benguael on the Western Coast of Africa; Mozambique, from the Bay of Lourenço Marques to Cape Delgado; Goa with its dependencies, and Macao, in Asia. In Oceanica, there remains to us the territory of Timor.

The Archipelago of Cape Verd forms with the establishments in Portuguese Guinea, the rich Province of Cape Verd. It produces coffee, sugar, brandy, molasses, cotton, indigo, oil, salt, leather, wax, ivory, iron, lead, and tobacco. Despite its great fertility, this province has not attained the desirable degree of prosperity, on account of the drouths, which have often produced the most lamentable famines. The home-country has, by reason of this almost periodical scourge, been compelled to submit to considerable sacrifices. These general drouths are due principally to the want of rain. To lessen the effects of the evil, efforts have been made to extend arboriculture; but the prejudices of ignorance have been great hindrances to the administration. The various trees fit for use in building are beginning to fail, and fire-wood does not exist in sufficient quantities. Fruit trees, such as the Cocoa-nut tree, the fig tree, the orange tree and others, are to be met with.

The game is confined to a few hares, quails and heath-cocks. The various domestic animals of Europe are sufficiently numerous. The climate is good in the elevated districts, but it is unhealthy along the coast, at Santiago and in the Island da Praia, it is even dangerous. The area of the archipelago is about 127 square leagues. The population amounts to about 100.000 inhabitants. The geographical position of their islands makes them a kind of intermediary between Portugal and her other posessions in Africa, and they assume an exceptional place. The Province of CapeVerd is under the orders of a governor-general In regard to public instruction, much progress has been made ; for in 1855, there were only a few schools, whereas, in 1863, there was established a lyceum, in the Island of S. Thiago. There were, moreover, 40 schools, of which 9 were for girls. The curriculum in the lyceum consists of theology, philosophy, Latin, French, elementary mathematics. naval tactics and drawing.

The Financial administration is confided to the "Finance Committee, which has delegations at Bissau and Cacheu in Guinea. There are Custom Houses in all the Islands, as well as at Bissau and Cacheu, and 7 fiscal posts in Guinea. As regards the judiciary, the province forms two districts, dependent on the "Court of Appeal" in Lisbon. A Bishop is at the head of the insular hierarchy. For defense, there is a batallion of Chasseurs, composed of 20 officers and 506 rank and file. The control of the maritime service is placed in the hands of the port captains in each Island.

The Province of St. Thomas and Prince comprises St. Thomas, Prince and the fort of St. Jean Baptiste in the coast of Mina. It is very fertile, but its climate is dangerous to Europeans. Its prosperity was formerly great on account of its extensive commerce in sugar, however, this industry has been destroyed by the competition of Brazil. Besides sugar-cane, an excellent coffee is produced. Although corn, vegetables, potatoes and other fruits of the soil are easily raised, the progress of agriculture has not been very great, owing to the want of labor and of capital. The culture of coffee and cocoa is the most developed, owing, without doubt, to the little labor requisite for these articles. Cinnamon grows naturally, ginger is gathered equal in quality, to what is known to diggers under the name of *Curcuma:* the Dandé palm gives an oil which is employed in the manufacture of an excellent soap; the wild indigo of St. Thomas is better than that in Cape Verd, yellow cotton grows along the whole coast. The public works have not been neglected, especially those which relate to the Sanitary Condition of the Island of St. Thomas. Work is constantly going on, for the drainage of the marshes that occasion so much malaria in the Island. This colony demands constant efforts for the removal of the obstacles which prevent the development of its natural riches. Revolts and discords have, at times, nearly ruined it, and the laziness of its inhabitants has rendered it unhealthy, on account of their inattention to sanitary measures.

The province is under the orders of a governor resident in St. Thomas, assisted by a subaltern governor in Prince. It forms part of the jurisdiction of the Court of Loanda. As regards ecclesiastical matters, it is under the administration of the Patriarch of Lisbon. There are 9 parishes in St. Thomas, 1 in the Island of Prince, and 1 in that of St. Jean Baptiste d'Ajuda. The schools are on an excellent footing. A garrison of about 400 men serves as defence. The sanitary service is placed in the hands of 5 surgeons and 3 pharmacians, assisted by a company of military infirmarians. The superficies of St. Thomas is estimated at 270

square miles, and that of Prince at 72. The population in this
province has greatly increased. In 1844 St. Thomas contained
only 8,169 inhabitants; in 1867, the number had risen to 16,513.

The vast province of Angola is bounded on the north by the
Ambriz and the Congo, on the east by various Savage Kingdoms,
on the South by the sandy deserts of Cape Negro, and on the
west by the Ocean. It extends along 850 Kilometres of Coast,
and embraces 85,000 square Kilometres of area. Its condition
is much more satisfactory than that of the Colonies of which we
have just spoken, and the Colony would be yet more prosperous if
its tranquillity were not disturbed by frequent insurrections,
which paralize its commerce. After quiet has been restored,
by means of difficult and costly expeditions, the fine possessions
always resumed its vigour.

The civil and military adminstration comprises 28 arrondisse-
ments, subordinate to the governors of Benguéla, Mossamedes
and Ambriz. Public instruction does not require much reform.
There is at Loanda a seminary destined for the education of
missionaries. and attended, on the average, by 180 students.
The hygienic service is confided to a staff of 107 medical officers.
There are Custom Houses at Loanda, Benguela, Mossamedes
and Ambriz. The city of St. Paul de Loanda is the seat of the
Court of appeal composed of a President, 2 Counsellors and a
Royal procureur. Angola forms a Bishopric, the seat of which
is at Loanda, and is divided into 20 parishes. The military administration is directed by the governor-general of the province,
who is the head of the armed force. This force forms an effective of 2,082 men. The irregular troops comprise 2 battalions
of volunteers, and 28 companies distributed throughout the ar-
rondissements.

Like all the Portuguese colonies in Africa, that of Angola is
very rich in the productions of the vegetable kingdom. Cotton
succeeds remarkably well, especially along the sea, and requires

only the trouble of planting it: two crops may be raised in the year.

Sugar-cane of an excellent qualtity grows very well in the interior, upon the banks of the rivers; indigo is to be met with everywhere; the culture of rice is susceptible of considerable development. Cocoa-nuts, wheat, tobacco, coffee, the Dandé palm, the arachide, copal gum and tamarinds are produced. The tobacco is of superior excellence, as is also the coffee, which is often preferred to that of Brazil. Such varied and numerous products must make this province incalculably valuable in the course of time. But labor, capital, the means of transportation and wise measures in the colonial administration are the first necessities.

The mineral treasures are not inferior to the others; but they are not yet explored. There have been discovered mines of iron, sulphur, salt, nitre and copper.

The chief exports are brandy, cotton, palm oil, coffee and gin-yuba in the grain. The exportation of cotton has increased from 29,488 kilogrammes in 1859, to 25,438,400 kilogrammes in 1867. Previous to 1868, Portugal was compelled to assist this colony, by sending money to make up the annual deficit. This has quite disappeared.

Mozambique, extends along more than 300 leagues of coast, from Cape Delgado to the Bay of Lourenco Marques. Besides the Islands of Cape Delgado, and the Island of Mozambique, this province comprises the vast territories of Rios de Sena, or Zambezi, and of Sofala, Inhambane and Lourenco Marques. Its area is about 4,000 square leagues. It is bounded on the North, by Zanguebar coast; on the East, by the Indian Ocean; on the South, by Caffraria, and on the West by unexplored countries. Its population is estimated in the absence of complete statistics, at 70,000. The province is divided into seven military districts, viz: Mozambique, Quilimane, Téte, Sofala,

Inhambane, Lourenco Marques and the Islands of Cape Delgado. The state of public instruction leaves much to be desired, but attention is being paid to it. The service of public hygiene is confided to a staff of seventeen medical men. There is a military hospital at Mozambique. Custom Houses are established at Mozambique and Quilimane, Ibo, Inhambane, Lourenco Marques and Angoche.

The judicial administration comprehends two tribunals subject to the Court of Appeal at Goa. A Prelate who is subject to the Archbishop of Goa, rules church matters. The Governor-general of the province has the command of the military. Reinforcements have frequently been sent for the purpose of maintaining tranquillity.

Cereals, fruits, meats, poultry, fish, gold iron, copper and wood are the productions. The forests, tenanted by elephants, offer great inducements for the investment of capital, especially since they are traversed by rivers. Coal-measures are found in various parts. The agricultural industry is not very flourishing. Many efforts have been made by the government to promote the culture of cotton.

In 1863, Sr. Mendes Leal said, in a report on the provinces beyond the sea; "The future of the Province of Mozambique, perhaps the richest of all, consists in the opening of the Isthmus of Suez, that gigantic work which was the thought of the great Affonse d'Albuquerque, and which is to-day the glorious emblem of the perseverance of a man, whose name will remain forever allied to the glories of this century." The Isthmus is open, and we have to wait for colonial reforms alone, to witness the immense development of which Mozambique and its regions are susceptible. A steamship line between this country and the metropolis would soon effect great advantages to both. A rapid and regular communication is of the first necessity.

Portuguese India, comprises the territories of Goa, Damao

and Diu. That of Goa has an extent of 20 leagues from the Fort of Tiracal, in the North, to Cape Rama in the South; and of 15 leagues from the Western coast of Hindoostan to the mountains of Gates. It is bounded by the British posessions and the sea. It is composed of a part of the continent and of islands formed by estuaries and rivers. The principal island is that of Tissuart, on which the city of Goa is built; it forms with the continent two ports, which can receive ships-of-the-line.

The area of the Portuguese territory in India is about 2,075 square kilometres. Its population amounts to 438,600 Europeans, Asiatics and Africans. The Governor-general resides at Goa. In accordance with the re-organization of the armed force decreed in 1871, the garrison consists of a battery of artillery, a corps of police and an expeditionany battalion. The fiscalisation of the customs, which was formerly in the hands of the army, is undertaken by a special corps. There is at Goa, a Professional Institute, very useful for industrial and commercial instruction, as well as for the study of pilotage. As regards public instruction, Goa is the best provided of all the colonies. The sanitary service is excellent, military hospitals are to be found at Goa, Damao and Diu. The administration of justice is subordinate to the Goa Court of Appeal. Goa is the seat of an Arch-bishop, who bears the title of " Primate of the East." This province, the theatre of the great deeds which reflected so much honor on Portugal, is very rich in productions of the soil. Salt, cocoas, fruits, pepper, sugar-cane, coffee the cereal, tea and cotton are produced. Rice, maize, spices and aloes abound. There are mines of iron in the Bardez district and in other localities. The forges of the country employ several hundred workmen. The culture of all these natural riches is being developed every day.

The establishment of Macao, in China, and the Portuguese territory of Fimor, in Oceania, form one province. The population, which amounts to 35,000 inhabitants, is for the greater part Chinese. According to the relation of Baron de Hübner, there are no more than twelve families of pure Portuguese blood in Macao, if we except the various employees of the government. The "coolie brokers" alone, prospered as well as the keepers of the gambling houses, when that illustrious diplomat traveled in China. But now, thanks to the measures taken, that state of affairs no longer exists. The traffic in coolies has entirely ceased. According to Baron de Hübner, the Chinese are prospering; they have established themselves in the handsome houses formerly occupied by the Portuguese. The causes of the decadence of commerce, as far as it concerns the Portuguese, are to be found in the powerful competition of the Chinese, and the opening of the treaty-ports. Macao had been, since the middle of the 16th century, the fountain of Catholicism for the extreme East.

During modern times, Portugal has sent to Macao, as governors, distinguished men, such as the Vicomte da Praia Grande, Vice-admiral Sergio de Souza, Vicomte de Saint Janerario and many others, whose efforts have been employed in ameliorating the administration of the province. Tea is now exported by the Yang-tse-kiang ports, instead of by Canton and Macao.

It was at Macao, that Camoens composed the poem, the renown of which will shine to the end of centuries.

Macao is the seat of a Bishop. The judicial administration is subject to the Court of Appeal at Goa.

The climate is salubrious and the territory fertile, but the cyclones cause ravages of a frightful extent. Macao has been open to all nations since 1845.

One can recognize that colonization and indigruous labor are the two principal questions connected with the future of the Portuguese posessions. It had often been observed, that the labor of the natives can lend only a feeble assistance to the efforts of the Europeans, on account of their lazy and vicious habits; and unfortunately these failings have increased since the abolition of slavery. Although that abolition is a triumph for the principles of humanity, its results will remain deplorable, if such a fact is not accompanied by other measures, which might operate a complete transformation in the slave, by changing him into a useful and educated citizen. One method, which has been tried, with some good results for agriculture in certain colonies, is that of the privileged concession of lands for a very small rental to the States. The privileges accorded to individuals or to societies, are: the free importation during the space of ten years, of all the materials, machines, etc., destined for the cultivation of the earth and the transport of goods; this exemption as far as steam and sailing vessels are concerned, extends to only those which are intended for coasting, or which are to be used on colonial rivers. There is, moreover, an exemption for the cotton which the concessionaire imports during those ten years, as well as special facilities for having armaments for the defence of the agricultural establishments in these lands which are under the surveillance of the government. These privileges cease when the concessionaires have allowed five years to elapse before they commence cultivating. To encourage agriculture still more, the government has been authorized to lay out great sums in the purchase of the cotton harvests and of agricultural machines; and in bestowing during the space of ten years, six annual rewards on the cultivators; one of four contos, one of two contos and four of one conto of reis.

Let us now examine the figures of the last colonial budget. The receipts of the provinces beyond the sea are estimated for 1875–1876 at 2,027,154,220 reis, and the Expenses at 1,930,-163,828 reis. There is therefore a surplus of 96,990,392 reis, and it is a very flattering result, when we consider that a few years ago, the mother-country had to made up the deficit in the Colonial budget.

It is the commencement, so to speak, of a most prosperous
(8)

future. To convince ourselves of the truth of this, we have only to compare the budgets of the different provinces for the past decade.

For St. Thomas and Prince.

Year.	Receipts.
1863–1864	24,725,882, reis
1874–1875	97,086,000 "

For Angola.

1863–1864	258,104,489 reis.
1874–1875	542,234,000 "
Increase,	284,129,511 "

The indirect imports produced as follows:

1863–1864 to 1869–1870 (average)	184,324,240 reis.
1874–1875	400,360,000 "
Increase,	216,035,760 "

When a colony in the space of five years only, by the regular movement of its commerce, doubles the custom revenues, it is evident that it contains in itself the greatest elements of life and of wealth.

Mozambique.

1863–1864	100,429,000 reis.
1874–1875	247,713,000 "
Increase,	147,284,000 "

We see then that the receipts of the provinces beyond the sea have now a surplus of about 97 contos of reis, over the expenses, in which expenses are included the subsidies for the payment of interest and for the retiring of the capital of 1,750 contos raised for the purchase of the ships-of-war, to which we alluded, when speaking about the marine. This sum of 97 contos shows an actual increase of 5 per cent. on the receipts. It should be remarked that, during 1857–1858, there was a deficit of 182 contos in the colonial budget, and consequently, there were resources for only four-fifths of the expenses, and whereas the expenses were estimated at only 975 contos in 1857–1858, they amount up, in this present year, to 1,930 contos, that is to say, to twice the former sum. Moreover the receipts have increased from 792 contos to 2,027, almost treble! If the increase in revenue had followed the same proportion, in the mother-country, we should now have more than 28,000 contos of revenue; but to have obtained that result, it would have been necessary to have avoided civil wars ; the imposts should always have been borne equally by the "contribuables," landed property and industry should not have remained for so long a time without paying in proportion to their values, the taxable articles should have clearly designated by the proper authorities (the assessment even now being defective,) and finally it should not have been permitted to have electoral affairs settled by the various parties, in a manner detrimental to the public treasury!

These abuses have nearly disappeared, but it is not the less true that their existence prevented the public revenues from becoming trebled, instead of doubled, in the space of 20 years.

The Portuguese Colonies then are on the high-road to prosperity. The impetus has been given, and the most far-sighted statesmen are neglecting nothing, that they might derive from the Colonies, the immense resources which they contain. Direct and regular communication by steam, between the two coasts of Africa and Lisbon, the developement of the public works, the questions relating to labor and to emigration, deserve the particular attention of the Portuguese administration.

We are informed that there is a project on foot, to raise a large loan for public works and improvements in the Portugese possessions. To those who would wish to obtain a more exact account of the state of our colonies, we should recommend the examination of the last report presented to the cortes. It contains

of 189 pages and was skillfully prepared by the present minister
of Marine, Andrade Corvo.   As our language is not generally
spoken, it is possible that a French or an English translation
will soon be brought forth.   Such translation would be of great
service to the honor and reputation of Portugal.

ʀELATIONS OF ᴘORTUGAL WITH THE
ᴜNITED ꜱTATES.

A personage who has contributed the most, of late years, to the amelioration of public matters in Portugal, wrote in 1870, concerning North America in the following terms: "The United States, the most striking manifestation of Democratic power, become connected more and more with the world, by their political and commercial relations. Launched between two great oceans, the Atlantic and the Pacific, North America unites itself on one side with Western Europe, in manners, civilization and commerce, as in its democratic aspirations; on the other side, it extends its maritime and commercial influence to Oceania and to Asia; and by joining its interests with those of Russia, large conquests are being prepared for civilization. In this manner, the United States meets Europe on the East and the West. Accustomed to look upon liberal democracy and the republic as being intimately connected with one another, public opinion (the supreme arbiter of all public resolutions in the United States) appears to give an equal value to the victories of modern ideas, and to those of the republic.

But public opinion in the United States should understand that in Europe there are traditions which it would be impossible to efface; that the various forms of government are the consequence and the result of those traditions, and that liberty, democratic progress and national independence, are not the less real even without a republican exterior."

The government of the nation by the nation can take place

in a constitutional monarchy as well as in a republic. Is it necessary to cite examples? We cast our eyes around on the horizon of Christendom, and we find that there is absolutely more liberty in the limited monarchies than in the republics. England, Portugal, Belgium, Holland and others, present an aspect of tranquil prosperity. Whereas France, Spain (lately a republic), the South American Republics and Mexico, appear torn by the worst of tyranny, that of demagogues. We need not enter into a detail of the grievances under which those unhappy countries labor. They are too recent to require recapitulation. Portugal, possessing the most extensive liberties, could not become any other than a monarchical country; and it is in preserving, henceforward, the form of government she has had for so many centuries, that her independence remains assured. As for ourselves, and it is not, perhaps, merely a personal opinion we have the conviction that if the republic were proclaimed at Lisbon and at Madrid upon a solid base, the same day would commence the danger against our nationality; for the republics would, in time, become one.

In what a state are the former Spanish colonies, for the most part! Without dwelling on the very unfortunate financial situation of several, do we not see the parties at conflict with one another during the presidential elections; and the ambition for power, at any price, a permanent cause of demoralization. The personal and the party interests are deemed to be of the greatest value in the midst of these disorders. Better, we say, to preserve and guard carefully the monarchical principle in all the countries, in which it has been found possible to conciliate political traditions in a profitable manner with the wise exigencies of modern ideas. There, in a word, can be seen reigning together, without the least antagonism, order and liberty. Portugal is monarchical for the same reason that the United States are republican; the aim of the institutions is almost identical.

The two countries, under a political aspect, are united by a sort of affinity, which we would be wrong to overlook. Thus brought into contact by a natural sympathy, there remains to them only to find out the best means for developing their commercial relations.

Portugal is proceeding gradually to the arrangement of her tariff in a liberal sense; the reforms thus far adopted have produced good results. She has not exaggerated the protection due to her industries, and she has well understood that the elements forming the balance of commerce, namely, the imports and the exports have the tie of reciprocity in such a way, that, to favor the one gives, at the same time life to the other. Moreover, it should be remembered that Portugal being essentially an agricultural country, the exchange of her natural products becomes easier and more extended with "consuming" countries, the wealth of which comes, in a special manner, from their cheaper and better manufactures. Some years ago, we abolished the differential dues levied on various nations, and made them uniform, requiring only that there should be reciprocity. This measure was, for a long time, violently opposed, under the pretext of giving protection to Portuguese navigation, which did not remain the less stationary. Protection did not cause it to grow at all. The only benefit derived, accrued to a few persons, interested in the monopoly. We are marching steadily and prudently towards the "school of Free Trade," in which, we think, all civilized nations will yet be united. Railroads, steam-navigation and the electric telegraph are charged with the first part of the game, the interests of nations, when better appreciated, will effect the rest.

As to what concerns Portugal and the United States, we believe that although their commercial relations are hindered at present by causes quite exceptional or accidental, these relations will become, in the near future, of a greater value. The culture of the wine in Portugal, as was remarked in the article on argiculture, has a great future before it. It would be a question of time merely, if immediate steps were taken, in the disposal of the available 1 000,000 hectares to which reference was made. Attention should be paid, moreover, to improving the present methods of wine-making. At present, Portuguese wines are subject to a smaller tax than before, owing to a law voted by the last Congress. It might be added, that the elevation of the tariff by the United States is a great obstacle to the development of American foreign trade. While the enormous debt charges left by the civil war continue to hang, like the sword of Damocles, over the American budget, it would be very difficult if not impossible, to diminish the custom-dues. We should not lose sight of the sustained efforts of the partisans belonging to the " Protectionist school," who are opposed to the free introduction of foreign products, no matter how much cheaper they may be, than the similar fabrics produced in their own country. How - ever, whilst reflecting on this present system, we should remember that the United States will not always be in the hands of the Protectionists. This nation had scarcely three millions of inhabitants in 1706; it now possesses over forty millions. In the near future it must become an immense market for our articles of commerce, when some of the markets, of Europe may be closed against us. Our country then has every motive for profiting of the commercial opportunities for a future magnificent trade on this side of the Atlantic. Immediate steps should be taken.

Annexed is a table of the actual state of trade between the two countries.

Statement of Commerce between the United States and Portugal, During the Fiscal Years ending June 30th, 1873, 1874, 1875.

COMMODITIES.		IMPORTS.				
		1873.		1874.		1875.
		Quantities.	Dollars.	Quantities.	Dollars.	Quantities.	Dollars.
FREE OF DUTY.							
Argols............pounds		575,625	59,482	706,676	72,742	716,538	76.731
Barks, Cork............			386,133		326,538		251,023
Chemicals			3,779		11,888		1,478
Coffee............pounds		1,452	221	"		5,252	790
Gums............pounds		109,718	29,577	60 984	13,702	54,820	11,018
Gypsum............tons				276	656		
All other articles............			1,000		5,835		34.285
TOTAL............			480,192		431,361		375.825
DUTIABLE.							
Chemicals............			538		797		3,034
Fruits of all kinds............			4,640		3,055		3,601
Iron and Steel, and Manufactures of.			13,751		3,769		1,038
Leather " "					9		
Jute " "			37				
Marble & Stone " "			314		154		812
Oils, Olive............			5,025				328
Salt............pounds		11,303,338	11,623	16,964,654	15,846	12,442,654	15,711
Silk, Manufactures of............					57		404
Spirits and Wines............galls		6.047	51,588		42,692		69,313
Wood, Manufactures of............			170				30
All other articles............			11,197		8 395		11,170
TOTAL............			98,883		74.774		105,037
TOTAL IMPORTS............			579,075		506,135		480,362

Statement of Commerce between the United States and Portugal, during the Fiscal Years ending June 30th, 1873, 1874, 1875.

DOMESTIC IMPORTS.

COMMODITIES.		1873. Quantities.	1873. Dollars.	1874. Quantities.	1874. Dollars.	1875. Quantities.	1875. Dollars.
Agricultural Implements			1,040		1,208		242
Breadstuffs, Indian Corn	bushels	26,203	18,700		"	oats 4,137	2,500
Wheat	"	131,129	212,392	300,301	453,218	1,595,014	2,070,234
Wheat and Rye Flour	bls	2,070	16,810	886	6,350	12,241	72,830
All other grain, etc.			420		205		"
Carriages and Cars			29,210		"		31,827
Clocks			16,679		17,967		"
Coal	tons	954	4,850	60	330		"
Drugs and Dyestuffs			7,562		{ 1,663		9,908
Fancy Goods			107		4,335		"
Fruits of all kinds			55		"		"
Hemp manufactures of			1,841		7,743		43,608
Ice	tons	610	2,350		"		"
Iron and Steel, manufactures of			2,424		1,651		2,115
Leather and " "			51		"		1,231
Naval Stores: Rosin	bls	5,220	22,787	5,824	23,390	8,881	28,298
Oils: Naphtha	galls	5,200	1,187	5,000	900	1,500	240
Illuminating	"	1,171,754	267,163	1,297,589	210,329	957,807	122,935
Perfumery			1,033		2,165		696
Provisions, Bacon and Ham	pounds	3,727	398		"	305	53
Beef	"	27,000	2,070	32,000	2,075		"
Lard	"	"	"	6,710	620		"
Pork	"	15,000	1,200	10,000	850	40,000	3,550
Scales and Balances			435		862		850
Spirits of Turpentine	gals	83	39		"		"
Tallow	pounds	334,442	31,875	78,164	6,049	300,053	26,603
Tobacco, Leaf	"	4,430,602	325,229	5,148,041	448,435	1,263,260	199,602
Wearing Apparel			5,000		"		2,500
Wood and manufactures of			205,207		362,102		196,606
All other articles			2,073		1,095		3,671
TOTAL DOMESTIC EXPORTS			1,180,187		1,553,042		2,820,099
The Foreign Exports amounted to			5,450		25,819		48,737

Taking into consideration the geographical situation of the port of Lisbon in regard to that of New York, the advantages of a direct and regular communication, by means of a steamship line, between Portugal and the United States have often been noticed. It is evident that the well known dangers and risk of the present Trans-atlantic routes would be greatly diminished, if the route by way of Lisbon were adopted. Of course, much remains to be done, in reference to the removal of the present obstacles to the realization of such a plan as would divert a portion of the present colossal trade between American ports and the ports of Great Britain, France and Germany, to the proposed channel. An effort was made, some time ago, to institute a line of steam-ships between New York and some Mediterranean ports, which was to touch at Lisbon and one of the Azores. But although the conditions of trade were deemed favorable to the project, the refusal of Congress to vote a subsidy was a serious check.

We believe that the question, concerning Portugal, is reserved for the future. When by the completion of our system of railroads, we are placed in easy and rapid communication with the rest of Europe, by the north of Portugal, instead of over the present line to Badajoz and Madrid, then can we discuss the problem of steam communication with New York in a practical manner.

In the interim, however, both sides should seek the means of developing their mutual relations. America should diminish her tariff dues to a great extent, some of which dues are particularly hostile to the importation of our productions; on the other hand Portugal should extend her viticulture and sericulture over the vast area which is at present entirely uncultivated, although found to be very available to these two branches of industry. The vegetable and the chemical products, which constitute so important places in the list of our exports to the United States,

must also be attended to. Before arriving at the epoch we desire so earnestly, it seems to us that every other circumstance
presents rather the expression of a praiseworthy desire than a
solid base. If it were otherwise, speculation, which is the touch-
stone of promising and lucrative enterprises, would have, ere
this, taken hold of the subject, without waiting for the prompting
of rhetoric.

It is our opinion that the moment is near at hand for proceeding
to the revision of the commercial Treaty drawn up thirty-five
years ago, between Portugal and the United States, and for
concluding another which will contain advantages for the two
countries.

The commercial policy of the Washington cabinet appears to
be dominated, at present, by the principle of not establishing,
as the principal basis of negotiations, the concession, in the absolute,
of the same treatment enjoyed by the most favored nation; there
are grounds for believing that the international arrangements, in
which the above sentiment is dominant, will be successively de-
nounced, thus leaving to the United States' government full
liberty to treat with any nation in such a manner that advantages given to one nation, may not be extended to others.

It is thus, that lately, in article 12 of the Treaty of Commerce with Belgium, signed March 8th, 1875, there is an addition to the terms of the corresponding article in the 1858 treaty,
according to which treaty neither of the high contracting parties
may concede any advantage to a third power, conditionally or un-
conditionally, without extending the same advantage to the other
contracting party. The alteration consists in there being added
to the aforesaid article 12, the following :

" If one of the two contracting parties notify the other of its
intention to annul the said article, its effects will cease one year
following the notification, the other articles of treaty remaining
in force, etc."

In the interests of the industries of Portugal as of the United

States, we think it would be necessary to add an article to the treaty formerly made, concerning the protection of trade-marks, a measure so much the more urgent as it is known that Portuguese wines have fallen into disrepute, because of the Hamburg, Cette and other fabrications.

The contents of article 15 of the treaty now in force between Belgium and the United States might serve as a guide for us. It would be perhaps, necessary to establish new dispositions for the transit of merchandize in the two countries.

Concerning the differential navigation dues, there was effected between Portugal and the United States, posterior to the 1840 treaty, an arrangement, by which such dues no longer exist. It would perhaps be possible to obtain, in future negotiations, that certain articles of Portuguese export to the United States may be admitted here on better conditions, compensation being given, of course, on our side.

These indications can have no other than a very general character, as there must be a certain reserve in questions of this nature. It appears to us that during the coming International Exposition in Philadelphia, the situation and the necessities of the great American market, in relation to the consumption of the principal Portuguese products, should be carefully studied, as well as the advantages which Portugal might obtain from many articles of American industry. Such a study would certainly deserve the particular attention of the members of the Portuguese Centennial Commission, and it should bring about a new arrangement between the two countries.

EPILOGUE.

We shall now make a few general remarks upon the present interior and exterior condition of the country.

In Portugal there are indeed no dynastic parties; and the liberal family does not contain the elements of demagogy in its organization. In truth, there is no fear of party extremes, in regard to either ultramontanism or socialism. The liberals of the party termed "regenerating," aided by the ancient chartists, constitute the conservative element, as they wish to preserve the already existing institutions, at the same time introducing reforms in a gradual manner.

Those called historico-progressists are the most important adversaries to the regenerators. They possess almost the same ideas as to the administrative material, but they desire to go further than their antagonists in the realization of political reform. At any rate, the historic progressive party has not rendered less service to the country than the regenerators. Both deserve well of the Commonwealth.

A short time ago, a group headed by the Bishop of Vizeu when in power, applied the principle of administrative economy; but they do not appear to have met with much success in their purpose, because, although they diminished certain charges on the State and made reductions in the salaries of the State-employees, on the other hand they contracted heavy loans abroad, during their term of office. The situation was indeed critical, but in the means they adopted for the purpose of ameliorating it they did not display great financial ability.

The reformers were certainly distinguished for eminence, patriotism and independent character. The Bishop it must be conceded, possessed the best intentions, but he allowed himself to be carried away by circumstances.

If the partisans of the Infant, D. Miguel dream of the restoration of an absolute monarchy, it is because they are attached to their traditions, rather than that they are convinced of the practicability of their ideas.

Politics in Portugal have often been suited to mere personal convenience. But lately the various principles have gone to the limits of the political field and the parties seem to tend to a regular and profitable organization. Of course logic ends by triumphing over everything, and political morality must, in the future, become more respected than it has been in the past.

The former party leaders are being gradually shelved. In Portugal as in the United States, politicians constitute an impediment. The elections are epochs of corruption, and the intervention of the authorities in them is the worst defect in our administration. Such abuses deserve to be corrected. The electoral law is good, but those who should watch over the faithful application of it, are sometimes culpable. It is perfectly admissible that the government should morally assist the members of its party, in the electoral labors, but it ought not to bring influence to bear through its agents. Let us hope that, endowed with full liberty, the press attacking such proceedings in a sincere manner, an end will be put to them.

Since 1851, civil wars and revolts have ceased in Portugal, although a famous General in 1870 conceived a plan of revolt, which assuming insignificant proportions utterly failed. This general, however brilliant his qualities may have been, did not make an effort of any great importance, and he was soon compelled to remit the administration into other hands, accepting, at the same time, a lucrative mission abroad.

Not many years ago, the finances of the country were in a wretched condition, although the resources of the country were ample. The evil arose in part from bad financial administration and from an anticipation in regard to giving to Portugal that material development, without which the fountains of its natural wealth would remain dormant. The nation has been compelled at times, to resort to credit, thus obtaining capital, indeed at a high rate of interest; but the country may justly claim the honor of never having failed to meet its engagements. Portugal, even in the direst distress of its treasury, has never had recourse to violent means to obtain relief, such as the circulation of paper-money, or the creation of excessive imposts. In tight times, the rights of the State-creditors have always been respected, but the public functionaries, who are already moderately paid, give up a precentage of their salaries. Indeed the Portugese bonds display an upward tendency in the marts of the world, thanks to good management, peace and the influx of money brought back by rich traders from Brazil. In a word, the public credit is being strengthened on all sides.

Portugal is now blessed with the most liberal laws. · The one in reference to the press is worthy of mention. The only formality required is, that the name of the editor must be given to the civil authorities.

Undoubtedly Roman Catholicism is predominant; but all the other creeds are tolerated, not the slightest coercion being brought to bear on any individual. This policy is, in our opinion, the wisest that could have been adopted by Portugal. Instead of being injurious to the interests of Rome, it is the truth that our Holy Church prospers most vigorously wheresoever there is religious liberty. We can point to the spread of the true faith in England and in the United States as a proof of our statement. By all means let us keep the Church and State separate, but let us not forget to render unto Cæsar, the things that are Cæsar's, and unto God, the things that are God's.

The Chamber of Peers is not constituted in accordance with the nature and the tendencies of the other liberal institutions, now existing in Portugal. In this age of the world, the hereditary principle cannot be adhered to. Sometimes it happens that the heir of a Peer enters upon the important duties connected with this chamber, without possessing the independence or the capacity so essential to one that desires to exercise this high mission. The illustrious Count de Casal Ribeiro proposed, a short time ago, the reform of that chamber of which he is himself a member. But his plan contains a great defect, since it retains the hereditary principle, thereby failing to possess the requisite thoroughness.

Nevertheless it is a step in advance, as it promises more guarantees concerning the competency and the personal worth of future Peers, than can be found under the existing arrangements. It is possible that the moment has not yet come, when a Senate composed of elective and of nominated Senators would be effective. Reforms, it must be admitted, cannot be introduced in a sudden manner. But between a purely elective Senate and a chamber of hereditary Peers, there must be a "juste milieu." That juste milieu, we think, has not been reached by Count de Casal Ribeiro. That statesman has effected great good by establishing certain categories of distinguished personages, such as admirals, generals, leading judges, the higher ranks of diplomacy, etc., from which categories the sovereign might select his future Peers. He makes it essential that the heir of a Peer in order to gain access to the chamber, must have reached his thirtieth year, be included in one of the categories above mentioned, and at the same time possess a certain income. Let us finish with the hereditary Peerage, as has been already done with the principle of "entail," respecting, however, the rights of the immediate heirs. All perceive the necessity of reorganizing the higher chamber on a basis more consonant with the interests of the nation, than the present one.

That Ministerial responsibility, now existing only in name is another point worthy of attention, and the settlement of which is so much the more indispensable, because, in Portugal, the person of the King is inviolable, the Secretaries of State being responsible for all the acts of the executive power.

A reform in the Court of Accounts has become necessary, and perhaps a more thorough organization of this tribunal might be adopted advantageously. The Tribunal of Accounts should be superior to the government, for the simple reason that it has the duty of revising the expenditures of the different departments; it receives all the documents concerning the control. Honesty is the rule in the various Portuguese departments. Indeed we never meet with an example of a minister becoming enriched at the expense of the public treasury, nevertheless we must guard against the defects inherent in our nature, and the country, at any rate, has an interest in knowing whether the expenditures of the public revenue are subject to a vigorous fiscalisation. Naturally all the appropriations should be devoted to the objects for which they were intended, and all the items arranged before an order for payment is given. As for the constituent organization of the court, the members must be independent in their power, and superior to party strife. No one would dispute the utility of such a tribunal, charged with examining whether the budget-receipts are duly employed, and the appropriations not exceeded. Such should be the important powers of a court constituted for the purpose detailed in the preceding lines, in all countries.

The principle of association, which has been so profitable in other nations, has not yet received in Portugal the attention which is due to it.

The abolition of the death penalty for civil crimes, which abolition cast so much honor on the Portuguese name, instead of increasing diminished the number of crimes. This fact should strengthen the opinion of those who maintain that the spread of religion and of instruction can effect more than the dread spectre of death.

As the President of the United States mentioned in his last Message to Congress, slavery exists no longer in the Portuguese possessions. The complete emancipation recently decreed abolishes every kind of servitude. The nefarious traffic in coolies by way of Macao is now extinct, thanks to the wise measures adopted by the present minister of Marine and Foreign affairs, Senor Andrade Corvo.

Much could be said concerning the improvements introduced into Portugal during the last few years, but the limits we have determined upon prevent us from doing more than citing the principal facts which occur to us. The Portuguese, whilst desirous of obtaining free institutions have not forgotten the advantages of order. They regard the dynasty now reigning with much affection, on account of the numerous favors bestowed on the nation by the present and the preceding sovereigns. D. Pedro V. was a model of great virtues, both as a king and as the head of a family. The present king knows well how to gain the sympathy of his people.

In a memorable letter addressed to the noble Duke de Loulé, then President of the Cabinet, whose recent death was deplored by all his countrymen, the King endeavored to put an end to the fears of his people. who imagined that he would accept the Spanish crown, and in this manner, destroy the independence of his country. He made use of the following phrase, "I was born a Portuguese and I will die a Portuguese."

Portugal contains a galaxy of illustrious names. If we have not, as in the past, men of exalted genius, such as the Infante D. Enrique, Vasco da Gama, Magalhaes Camoens, Alphonsus d'Albuquerque, and the Marquis de Pombal, we can mention however, many distinguished names, the bearers of which have devoted their existence to the honor and profit of their country.

The Marshal-Dukes de Saldanha and Terceira, the Dukes de
Palmella and de Loulé; the Marquises de Sâ da Bandeira and
d'Avila et Bolama ; the Counts de Thomar and de Casal Ribeiro
(all of which titles were conferred after the revolution of 1834,
although some of the honored personages already belonged to
the nobility) Fontes Pereira de Mello, Braamcamp and many
others have rendered signal services to their country. We might
add the names of José Estevan de Magalhaes and of Alexander
Herculano, both of whom are known at home and abroad ; the
former as a parliamentary debater, the latter as an erudite historian.   Rebello da Sylva, Mendes Leal, Andrade Corvo, Rod-
rigue Sampayo, Antonio de Serpa and Latino Coelho, have
contributed and do still contribute to the splendor of Portuguese
literature and journalism.

    We should not pass over the name of the noble Marquis de
Sa da Bandeira, without failing to refer to the services he per-
formed against slavery in our possessions beyond the sea.   It
was he who obtained the complete emancipation of the enslaved
blacks, thus gaining for Portugal the praises of the whole world.
President Grant, in his late message to Congress, expressed the
opinion of all his countrymen, when he eulogized the Portuguese
in regard to the matter.   We could compare the Marquis to the
lamented Lincoln and Charles Sumner, when we consider
his efforts in behalf of freedom.

    As we have seen, the liberal institutions are not yet complete;
but they are founded on a firm basis, and require only to be
faithfully adhered to, in order to produce the most beneficent
results.   Now that the finances have been arranged, the future
prosperity of Portugal is assured, as the efforts of all may be
directed henceforward to completing the system of railroads,
and to developing the colonies.   It will be necessary, however, to see that the ramifications of the administrative departments become more enlightened, and active.

Whilst speaking of that stability so necessary in the political administration, we ought, however, to add that this stability can never be brought about by any coterie, or by means of concessions, which could never emanate from strict morality.

In labor as well as in economy is found the true wealth of nations, as of families. Liberty is precious only when she contributes to the acquisition of the one or of the other. It is indispensable, therefore, that Portugal should be a land of, not only liberty, but industry and economy.

Portugal has maintained cordial relations with all the foreign powers; but there are some, the friendship of which is of the greatest importance to her. The first place is occupied by England, a country that has been, according to the Portuguese, their most faithful ally. The relations with Brazil and with Spain, are no less worthy of consideration. England great amongst the first nations of the globe, has always followed principles, which should serve as rules for free countries, and she has undoubtedly contributed the most to the perfecting of the human mind. Her moral force arises partly from her material power. Look at her prodigious commercial activity, her immense naval resources and the number of subject nations, which, beyond the British Isles, acknowledge her sway! We might particularize the magnificent empire of Hindoostan, and the superb colonies of Australia and of Canada. English interests with which the national greatness and prosperity are bound up, require that the brutal logic of might over right, should not be established in the world. Owing to the great distance of her possessions, she would find it difficult to retain them, even with the assistance of her squadrons, were the doctrine of "vae victis" introduced into the political relations of the world. It should be her aim to represent the rights of meum and teum in the councils of Europe. Let her but show the road to the spoliation of other countries, and she would find that she had been handling a two-edged

sword. Other nations would soon follow her example. Inflamed
by an eager lust after her rich dependencies, they would press
on to their conquest. Thus far she has adopted the policy we
have adverted to. Her moral influence in the politics of Europe
is great, owing to the comparative honesty of her conduct. This
influence is indispensable to her, if she desires to retain her foreign dominion.

Since the 18th century, England has rendered very great
services to Portugal. As soon as Portuguese autonomy was
fully established, consolidated and recognized, Spain became
the natural ally of Portugal, and the idea of closing the
whole Peninsula to whatsoever might be dangerous in regard to foreign interference was the cherished dream of several statesmen in both countries, chiefly towards the end of the
15th century. Events, however, followed one another, of such
a kind as to keep up a state of mutual distrust, and to provoke
a radical separation between the two nations, whose interests
should have brought about an intimate alliance. The domination of the Philips, which was the severest attempt against the
rights of the Portuguese, the revolution in 1640, the war for the
restoration of the Braganzas, the accession of the Bourbons of
France to the Spanish throne, the French Revolution and its
effects on Spain, and lastly the invasion of Portugal by the
Spaniards combined with the French, at the beginning of this
century, completed the antipathy of the one nation for the other.
In the absence of a good and solid alliance with our neighbors,
brothers by race, language and religion, and possessing, possibly,
the same aim, it was necessary to look for allies in another
quarter. The resolution of choosing Great Britain as our principal political ally was a wise one, inasmuch as there already
existed commercial relations between the two countries. Great
Britain was the chief consumer of our principal agricultural pro-

duce wines, and the chief market whence we derived our importations.

Despite the efforts of some factious men, Portugal is no longer the feudatory of England, as some of our adversaries once called her. It may be remembered that Great Britain disputed our right to certain possessions we claimed. The dispute was in regard to the Ilha de Bolama and other points in Guinea, and to the territories situated in the Bay of Lourenco Marques, on the Eastern coast of Africa. The two questions being submitted to arbitration, were gained by Portugal. The Marquis d'Avila, now President of the Chamber of Peers, defended the rights of his country in the affair of da Bolama. The arbiter selected for the Bolama question was the worthy President of the United States, General Grant. The affair of Lourenço Marques, which was managed by the Portuguese barrister, Paiva Manso, was submitted to the illustrious President of the French Republic, Marshal MacMahon.

On the other hand, the traditions of our political history and the important interests which unite us to the powerful English nation, are great reasons why we should not allow a sundering of our ties of friendship with England. An English writer, who traversed our country a short time ago, in speaking of this alliance, employed the following terms: "To us Portugal is, and always has been, an important part of Europe. The nation, small as it is, is not without potentiality of influence in European affairs. A Portuguese army is an admirable one. These facts should not be forgotten. This nation is our natural ally; the vigor, the self respect and that peculiar sturdiness of temper which we pride ourselves upon, are also Portuguese characteristics. The nation is to ourselves a friend, whose interests on this continent are our interests, whose enemies in a great war are quite certain to be our enemies, and who have left their own indelible mark on the page of history by virtue of some great and rare qualities, which happen to be those very qualities which have made of ourselves a great and famous nation."

May heaven grant that English statesmen will never forget these words, and that Portugal will always be able to flatter herself that she has remained faithful to the English alliance, an alliance that can be cemented only by the respect of their reciprocàl rights and duties.

Spain must eventually perceive the advantages of having her relations with us, in regard to commercial interests, rendered more intimate. Things are, undoubtedly, tending in that direction. The political state of Spain, when her civil war is once settled, will reach the same stage as ours is at present; free and independent of one another, as regards their respective autonomies, the two nations of the Peninsula must form, in the future, a sort of Zollverein.

Brazil is to Portugal, what the United States are to Great Britain. In North America, England sees her fairest daughter; and if the Americans are justly proud of the fabulous progress they have made during the past century, Great Britain can but flatter herself, when considering the prosperity and greatness of her former colonies. The battles of Concord and of Lexington, which gave the first victories to the Independent of the United States, cannot be regretted to-day by the English people.

If England throws a look of satisfaction towards the nation, her race and her genius have contributed to create, Portugal sees, with no less satisfaction, her former colony, Brazil, increasing in strength, and rapidly becoming one of the most flourishing empires in the world. She sees Brazil ruled by a member of the Portuguese Royal Family, a Prince of great capacity and virtue. The visit which S. M. D. Pedro II, Emperor of Brazil, proposes to make in a short time to the United States, will confirm the opinions entertained in this country regarding him.

Portugal must maintain only the most intimate relations with Brazil. Besides being the constant aim of the two governments, the friendly concourse of the one with the other, is kept up the more easily because of the mutual esteem that exists between the two nations.

France and Italy belonging to the same race, the Latin, are particularly dear to us. French policy, when the struggle was being carried on against England, mistrusting the temper of the Portuguese, never tried to gain allies in that quarter. However, the French are always welcome in Portugal, and their books fill our libraries almost exclusively. The French language has been, for a long period, familiar in Portugal, and it is from France that we still receive the greater part of the elements of knowledge which assist in improving the different branches of the administration. Customs, manners, etc., are always French importations with us.

Belgium is one of the countries we like to select as a model. We mention her frequently, and we admit the progress she has made in both moral and material improvements. It is needless to say that with all the nations of the world, Portugal is on some terms of friendship, and if her relations with them are not always very important in consequence they are at least carried on with great cordiality.

In the interests of just criticism, we have alluded to the errors and defects, which exist in our country, and from which even the best ruled countries are not exempt. The impartiality with which we have judged of events and institutions will have the merit of not causing, in the minds of our readers, any suspicion, when we speak with praise of public matters in Portugal. True patriotism, in our eyes, is that which seeks especially to inspire confidence, by placing truth above all other considerations.

We could not select a better mode of ending, than by making use of the memorable verse of Camoes.

Vereis amor da patria, nao movido
De premio vil, mas alto e quasi eterno;
Que nao e premio vil ser conhecido
Per um pregao do ninho meu paterno.

THE PORTUGUESE LAWS.

In speaking of Portugal and her laws after the introduction of the liberal regime, we should be wrong not to mention the name of the illustrious patriot, who was the intimate counsellor of D. Pedro IV., and the initiator of the great reforms which have been operating in the country since the victory of liberalism over absolutism. Portugal venerates the name of Mousinho da Silveira; for, if the cause of D. Pedro IV., signified the victory of good principles applied to the hereditary succession on the Portuguese throne, it was no less the triumph of the free institutions which the charter has bestowed upon us. The generous ideas as well as the energetic action of that illustrious man contributed to give to Portugal, a new epoch of aspirations, social and financial, the impress of which will always remain on the hearts of the Portuguese. The laws of May 16th, of July 30th, and of August 13th, 1832, shook, from top to bottom, the whole Portuguese social body and produced a complete revolution. It was by these three memorable laws, that Mousinho da Silveira traced the lineaments which so distinguish our present political organization. Perhaps these reforms destroyed many things, at that time which have not yet been replaced in a solid manner; but it is not the less true that the élan of the reformer was the starting point of all the ameliorations adopted afterwards by the liberal government for the organization of the administrative powers, and for the creation of the elements that reclaimed agriculture and industry, both of which had hitherto suffered through the atrophy produced by the want of an organic

development, so essential to the life of nations. As has been
very well said by a Portuguese writer, Sr. Teixeira de Vasconcellos, without the legislation to which we have just alluded, the
struggle between the two brothers, D. Pedro and D. Miguel,
would have had no important results; it would have been
regarded by the country, as a simple affair of personal ambition;
the courage of D. Pedro, the diplomatic efforts of the Duc de
Palmella, tne energy of Silva Carvalho, and the victories of
Marshals Saldanha and Terceira and of their companions in
arms, would not have been sufficient to vanquish the partisans of
D. Miguel.   It was Mousinho da Silveira, the friend and the
counsellor of D. Pedro, who destroyed the superannuated edifice
of despotism, by putting an end to the confusion then existing
throughout the civil and military administrations; by abolishing
certain feudal rights, hereditary employments, the too great
power of the clergy, the tithes and their abusive application,
many privileges, and by establishing, as much as possible,
equality before the law.   When speaking about Portuguese laws,
in general, it should be observed that they all bear the impress
of independence, and of a great tenacity in sustaining it against
powerful adversaries.   In the spirit of our legislation, one sees
pride and courage allied to softness of national manners. "Odiosa
restringenda" has never escaped our legislators.   During the
reign of D. Diniz, and of other Sovereigns, we see literature
honored highly; feudality disappearing before the free traditions
of the people, and before the enlightened justice of the Kings;
religion honored and the clergy protected, and the power of the
crown interposed vigorously in favor of the feeble against the
strong.

We might notice the zeal of princes, such as the Infante D.
Enrique and others, in pursuing the study of the arts and sciences,
and in making those branches assist enterprises, by which all
mankind has profited.   Finally, it can be observed, in the his-

tory of Portuguese law, that, as early as the 18th century, modern ideas already sought that development which philosophy was to bestow later on. They found their personification in the Marquis de Pombal, and prepared the Portuguese for the enjoyment of the social reforms, usually brought about by revolutions, without finding themselves stained with the crimes which disgraced France.

If one were to scrutinize the legal system of Portugal, it would be easily found that the majority of the laws are excellent; but they do not always meet with a strict interpretation. Time and enlightenment alone can correct the abuses. The people endowed with a supple character, and an intelligence which requires only to be cultivated, lend themselves, without difficulty, to the introduction of new laws. However, every nation has its special tendencies which the codes would be wrong either to overlook, or to destroy entirely, especially when these tendencies are not in opposition to the principles of civilization.

Our various judicial codes can be placed in the same rank as those of the most advanced nations. The present law concerning weights and measures had to contend with a strong opposition at the commencement of its application. Still such opposition was to be expected, as it is impossible to change the inveterate habits of centuries, without interfering with certain prejudices. We cannot be astonished that the metric system, although decreed on the 13th of December, 1852, was not generally adopted until the end of 1862. This did not arise from ignorance of the advantages to be derived from the innovation; for, on the contrary, the differences of the weights and measures were so great in the various parts of the kingdom, that the adoption of a uniform system for the whole country, besides taking into account the advantages of uniformity with the other countries that had accepted the metre, had become an absolute necessity.

There is understood under the designation, Special Instruction, the teaching of the Fine Arts, which is confided to the following establishments; the Lisbon Royal Academy of Fine Arts; the Oporto Academy of Fine Arts, and the Royal Conservatory of Lisbon. The first has six professors; in it the historical, the ornamental and the civil architectural styles of drawing are taught, as well as historical and landscape drawing, sculpture, wood engraving, and model drawing. The Oporto Academy, founded nearly a century ago, possesses four classes, viz: historical drawing and painting, civil architecture and sculpture, perspective and anatomy. The conservatory possesses a school of dramatic art, and one of music. Industrial and commercial instruction is given in two Institutes at Lisbon, and at Oporto. The courses are as follows: general instruction for workmen, the directors of factories, and masters and foremen of work-shops; for the con ductors of public works, conductors of machines, telegraphists, constructors of instruments of precision, without counting an elementary as well as a complete course in commerce. Agricultural education is divided into elementary and superior. There were founded in 1852 for the former, district farms; and in 1869 experimental stations were prepared in the various districts. An elementary course of agriculture is pursued in the lyceums. For the superior agricultural education, there is a general Institute of Agriculture, created in 1852, to which, in 1855, veterinary instruction, until then a distinct course, was added. In several districts, courses in agriculture and zoology are given without being obligatory. Without furnishing special skill, the aim has been to spread as much as possible, agricultural knowledge.

As regards scientific establishments, we should first mention the Lisbon Royal Academy of Sciences, which contains three principal classes, viz: natural sciences, mathematics and belles-lettres. The number of effective associates, according to the primitive statutes would be only eight. The number of super-numeries has been raised to twelve, of the honorary members also to twelve, and of the corresponding members to 100. Portugal appears to have the desire of giving a greater development to astronomic knowledge. It possesses three principal establishments, the Royal Observatory of Lisbon, the Observatory of Coimbra, and that of the Polytechnic School of Lisbon (in construction). That of Lisbon, which Portugal owes to the scientific labors and the liberality of the late Pedro V., was constructed on the plan of the Observatory of Palkowa. The Observatory of Coimbra, founded by the Marquis of Pombal, is annexed to the building of the University, and is destined chiefly to practical instruction in Astronomy, as comprised in the Faculty of Mathematics. Geodesic labors, of the actual state of which it is impossible for us to give an exact idea, by reason of want of space, are very far advanced in Portugal, and to those who would wish to have a complete knowledge of the works executed, or in course of execution—as far as hydrography is concerned, we can do nothing better than to indicate to them a book recently published in Portuguese, by M. Gerardo de Pery, under the title "General Geography and Statistics of Portugal and her colonies." Portugal possesses also two meteorological observatories, one in Lisbon, and the other at Coimbra; eleven ports of observation on the continent, and three in the adjacent islands. As regards museums of natural history, there are two, one in Lisbon, and one at Coimbra. The one in Lisbon possesses precious ornithological, conchological and geological collections of not only the country and its colonies, but also of other lands. We might mention the Museum of Archaeology, possessing already 1,600 objects of art; the Museum of the Academy óf Sciences, in which there is a rich numismatic collection, and finally the Industrial Museum, created by that indefatigable promoter of Portuguese industry, the late M. Fradesso da Silveira, formerly Royal Commissioner at the Vienna Exposition.

There are in Portugal four public libraries with a special donation from the state. The principal one is the National Library of Lisbon; the three others are at Evora, Braga and Villa Veal. Besides those we have just mentioned, the State possesses several other very important ones in the various scientific establishments. There are, of course numerous private libraries. The Academy of Sciences in Lisbon, the University of Coimbra, the Libraries of Evora and of Mafra possess very rare works and very ancient manuscripts. The National Library, in Lisbon, at present contains more than 300,000 volumes; that of the Academy of Sciences, 75,000, and that of the University, 58,000.

In the matter of benevolence, Portugal is one of the countries of Europe, in which it is exercised most'liberally. From the most distant times, there have existed institutions of charity such as the *misericordias*, charitable institutions of an origin especially Portuguese, the religious fraternities, poor-houses, foundling hospitals, etc., some of which (but by far the minority) created and sustained by the public treasury, and others maintained at the expense of private charity. Of these establishments of every kind, according to statistics collected in 1861, there were 9,861, possessing an annual revenue of more than 2,000 contos of reis. The number of those institutions has greatly increased since 1861. If the religious establishments were in the past the origin of the majority of the charitable institutions in question, it is not the less true, that, in more recent times, the spirit of charity, apart from all idea of religious fanaticism, has contributed by itself to the foundation of many of them. According to the table of statistics, there is one charitable institution to every 403 inhabitants. It might be remarked that perhaps charity has exceeded the real necessities of the times.

It has often been remarked how considerable is the number of illegitimate births in Portugal, and indeed the ancient laws, by giving to children born out of wedlock a somewhat regular and convenient position in the family, encouraged the abuse. The establishment of *rodas* also contributed much to illegitimate births among the populace; but since 1870, the advantage of suppressing the *rodas* in the Misericordias has been recognized, and whereas in 1870—1871, 2,559 children were exposed (in the Misericordias of Lisbon), the year after the number was reduced to 794, and in 1873—1874, to 357. We must therefore affirm that the abolition of the *rodas* in Portugal has been amongst others, one of the good measures adopted by the administration, to avoid the sad and often repeated abuses.

Two causes have been indicated as particularly favoring the current of Portuguese emigration towards the two Americas; repugnance to military force, and the desire after riches. At any rate, it is useless to add that there are everywhere, the same reasons which produce a penchant for expatriation. Germany probably affords the best example of this. In recent times, it is not the want of work which could explain or justify the mania for emigration, for the want of laborers for agriculture is being felt in some provinces, where the wages have been elevated. The temptations held out by the emigration agents constitute the principal motive. The larger portion is directed to Brazil, and the smaller to the United States. The provinces of Minho and Beira Alta, as well as the Azores, are the regions of Portugal, which furnish the largest contingent of emigrants. Accord-

(10)

ing to statistics which we have before us, the fifth part is composed
of minors of fourteen years.

Districts,	1874.
Aveiro, ...	925
Beja, . . .	2
Braga, ...	1,062
Braganza, . . .	19
Castello Branco, . .	3
Coimbra, ...	384
Faro, . . .	
Guarda, ...	37
Leiria, ...	12
Lisboa, ...	623
Pcrto, ...	2,900
Santarem, ...	2
Vianna, ...	638
Villa Real, ...	733
Vizeu, . . .	760
Angra, . . .	1,123
Horta, ...	273
Ponta Dagada. .	869
Funchal. . .	3
Total, . . .	10,368
Minors, fourteen years, ...	2,177

Total number for five years ending 1874, 46,828.

The mortality among the emigrants to Brazil is very great.
Of those who return home, the great majority return even poorer
than before, and often by the assistance of charitable institutions,
founded in Brazil by Portuguese. A relatively small number
acquire fortune, but only after hard labor and privations
of all kinds. Another class (and it is the very smallest)
obtain immense fortunes and remain in Brazil, forming the

most solid and important base of the Empire, without, at the same time, losing sight of the interests of their native land. Of late years, many former Portuguese residents in Brazil, have returned to Europe, taking with them considerable capital, which has served to augment the banking wealth of the country. According to the averages of the years, from 1871 to 1874, the annual mean of emigrants to Brazil is 11,689.

In the United States there exists a colony of Portuguese (chiefly in Massachusetts,) whose love of country always remains alive, and who return to their native heath, after having acquired some thousands of dollars. In 1872–73 there were 1,194 Portuguese emigrants to the United States; of this number 505 returned home, and twenty were naturalized.

Wine Regions.

For the better explanation of the Portuguese wine exhibition in London, the kingdom of Portugal was divided into eight wine-bearing regions, viz: 1. Douro; 2. Tras-os-Montes; 3. Minho; 4. Beira-Alta; 5. Beira-Baixa; 6. Extremadura; 7. Alemtejo; 8. Algarves.

First region, Douro. This region, divided into the sub-regions of Alto Douro, Superior Douro and Inferior Douro covers a superficies of 35,000 hectares, and is distinguished for a great variety of wines, which variety arises from the difference of geologic formations and altitudes. The annual average of wines produced is computed at 80,000 pipes, of 500 litres each, or 40,000,000 litres. The first quality, amounting to 10,000,000 litres, is chiefly exported, being the finest and most precious wines known in the markets of the world. The second quality is frequently equal to the first, and is sometimes mixed with it. Brazil is the principal market for this class, which mounts up to nearly 30,000 pipes. The third quality (30,000 pipes) is partly consumed in the country and partly reserved for reduction to brandy, which is added to the wines of the 1st and 2d qualities. The first quality is priced (per pipe of 500 litres) at about $55.00 gold, the second at $40.00, and the third at $22.40. The fine, generous port wine belongs to the first class.

Second region—Tras-os-Montes. This region formerly a province occupies a space of 1,111,556 hectares, and produces annually 66,600 pipes (500 litres each), of which some are exported to Spain, and others transported down the Douro to Oporto.

But the greater part is consumed in the localities of its production, or is distilled, being sold as brandy to mix with the Douro
wines. The red wines of Tras-os-Montes are chiefly pale, soft,
mild aromatic, more or less acidulous, and to a certain extent
alcoholic. There are some red wines, and in the Braganza
district white wines are met with.

PRICES.

1st quality—per pipe of 500 litres········$33.00
2d "   "   "   " ········ 22.50
3d "   "   "   " ········ 15.00

Third region—Minho. Minho occupies an area of 713,719
hectares, and produces 100,000 pipes or 50,000,000 litres. Its
wines, like all the others of Portugal, on account of the
singularity of their composition, are known under the denomination of vinhos verdes (tart wines) in opposition to vinhos
maduros (mellow wines). They are also named wines of enfor-
cado (vines tied to trees and growing up by them). The wines
of Minho are sour and biting, being thus distinct from all the
other wines of Portugal, but when well fabricated they make an
agreeable and healthy drink, being very refrigerant and diuretic.
Learned oenologists assert that the Minho wines, when well prepared, should have a large foreign consumption.

PRICES.

1st quality—per pipe of 500 litres········$27.50
2d "   "   "   " ········ 16.75
3d "   "   "   " ········ 11.00

Fourth region—Beira Alta. We have here 1,054,073 hectares,
producing 30,000 pipes or 15,000,000 litres. The wine produced near the river Dão is the first; it is largely bought up by
French merchants. The red wine of Beira Alta is thin, of little
color, soft, savoury, aromatic and mildly alcoholic.

PRICES.

1st quality—per pipe·······················$33.50
2d   "   "   ······················· 22.00
3d   "   "   ······················· 13.50

Fifth region—Beira-Baixa This region contains 1,343,600 hectares, and produces 140,000 pipes. With the exception of the famous red wines of Bairrada, white wines are generally produced, and are exported by Mondego (Figueira da Foz) to Brazil. The wines of Tortosendo, Alpedrinha, Valle de Prazeres rival the best foreign and domestic wines, and they are considered as being of the most precious types of Portugal.

PRICES.

1st quality—per pipe·······················$38.50
2d   "   "   ······················· 21.75
3d   "   "   ············ ············ 13.50

Sixth region—Extremadura. Extremadura contains 1,795,786 hectares, producing 190,000 pipes. We have the valuable red wines of Setubal, with the well known muscadine of St. Ubes, from the vineyards at Azeitao and Palmella; the red thick and durable Almada brands, the Lavradio, the saccharine Benavente, the Almeirim, the Chamusca, the white Carcavellos, the thin soft and acidulated Collares, the red and the white Termo, the Cartaxo, the Santarem, the Macão, the white Bucellas which is well known in foreign countries, the red and thick Torres-Vedras, the Arruda, the Cadaval, the delicious Caldas da Rainha e Alcobaça, the Leiria, the Batalha, the Ourem, the saccharine, alcoholic, and soft Torres Novas, and lastly the sweet, soft, pale and medium alcoholic Thomar.

PRICES.

1st quality—per pipe·················:·······$44.60
2d   "   "   ·········· ············ 33.75
3d   "   "   ······················· 22.25
4th   "   "   ······················· 13.50

The seventh region—Alemtejo contains 2,441,097 hectares, and produces 65,000 pipes. The production is small. There was an old proverb says that Alemtejo is a country of bad bread and bad wine (terra de mau pão e mau vinho). The best kinds are those obtained near Lisbon and Redondo, those of Cuba, Vidigueira, Villa de Frades, Ferreira and Serpa in the Beja district, and those of Elvas, Castello de Vide and Ribeira de Niza.

PRICES.

1st quality—per pipe $33.25

2d   "   " 22.25

3d   "   " 16.50

Algarves, the 8th district, contains 485,835 hectares, and annually produces 18,000 pipes. The wines of this region are not inferior to the wines of Madeira, Gerez and Malaga. The most esteemed are those of Javira, Olhão, Portimao and Lagos.

PRICES.

1st quality—per pipe $33.25

2d   "   " 26.50

3d   "   " 16.50

Whilst on this subject, we might append a few remarks concerning a recently disputed wine question in Portugal. It treats of knowing whether the common wines, named *de Pasto* may be included within twenty-six degrees of the Sykes proof-spirit instrument, without its being indispensable to extend the limit of the said wines to 30° or 34° of that alcoholic measure. Good authorities in Portugal maintain that the proposed change would be useless, as soon as a better system of fabrication should be adopted. This being the case, the prejudice, which is attributed to the English alcoholic scale, would no longer exist. But this opinion meets with opposition, and to know which side is right, it is evidently necessary to wait for future experience, which naturally depends upon radical change in the present methods of fabrication, which change at any rate has become essential. There are four points to which attention should be devoted: the wines should be fabricated, not according to the old defective methods, but after the recently improved modes; second, counterfeit wines should be prevented altogether; the bottling, corking and storage of the wines should be arranged in such a manner, that no injury would result from the necessary voyage, and last, a lowering of the tariff of the importing countries should be effected, so that our wines may not be handi-capped, when competing with the similar productions of other countries.

Colonial Treaty Lately Concluded.

After Portugal had gained the victory in the contest with England concerning the Bay of Lourenço Marquez, the government of the King did not hesitate to recognize that it was necessary to profit by the great resources which were offered to the commerce of Southern Africa and to civilization, by the magnificent position of the aforesaid bay, if it were known how to use, in a practical manner, all the resources of a port, which, on account of its proximity to the two republics of Transvaal and of the Orange river, is the most convenient for the imports and exports of the two States. The territories of those two republics are very rich in natural productions and in the most precious minerals attract from all parts of the world laborers, capital and intelligent persons able to explore and appraise them. The Bay of Lourenço Marquez is then destined to be the centre of a considerable traffic, when highways and a railroad have been constructed to connect the port with the interior regions.

According to a treaty recently made, it is believed that the importation and exportation of not only all meridianal Africa and Transvaal, but also of a large part of Orange Free State, will be conducted through the port of Lourenço Marquez. The bay by its situation and configuration, offers a broad anchorage ground, and a safe shelter to vessels of every tonnage, a facility to be so much the more appreciated, when we remember that storms and tempests are frequent on those coasts. The province of Mozambique cannot fail, by this arrangement concluded between Portugal and the Republic of Transvaal, to derive a development more extreme than heretofore, the republic and the province having been both placed on an equal footing, neither having any advantage over the other as regards facilities for transit, etc.

In the article devoted to the colonies, it was stated that a plan had been adopted, which was to lead to their more rapid development. We learn that the Government has asked the Chamber of Deputies for a capital of $5,000,000, destined for necessary public works on the two coasts of Africa. The said sum is to be devoted to the amelioration of the defective sanitary arrangements, and thereby to the reducing to a minimum of the fevers which so constantly arise; to shortening by canals the unnecessary length of the river navigation, caused by the meandering of the rivers, and at the same time, promoting the system of irrigation; to establishing light-houses, repairing the ports, adding quays, custom-houses, jetties and small forts, (the latter to serve, in cases of necessity, as aids to the military and naval forces); and lastly to opening routes connecting the interior with the coast, the want of which routes has hitherto retarded the exploration of mines, etc. It is beyond question that, by these measures, Angola and Mozambique must become extensive sources of wealth to Portugal, since capital and immigration will be attracted thither by such improvements.

THE DISCOVERY OF AUSTRALIA BY THE PORTUGUESE.

We believe that it would be interesting to reproduce, in this place, the translation of a letter written by a Portuguese navigator, Godinho de Eredia, from which letter, it would appear that, towards the end of the 16th Century (between 1597 and 1600), the Portuguese already knew of the existence of Australia under the name of "Terra do Ouro" (land of gold).

The letter was addressed by the cosmograph to the Viceroy D'Francisco da Gama, fourth Count da Vidigueira, who had taken possession of the government of the Portuguese Indies, 25th of May, 1597, which government he handed over to Ayres de Saldanha, 25th of December, 1600. Eredia addressed his sentiments of condolence to the Viceroy, on the occasion of the death of the third Count of Vidigueira, D. Vasco da Gama, grandson of the great Admiral. We might add that Godinho de Eredia died in 1615.

Translation of Letter:

Most Illustrious Sir:—Upon the arrival of the men-of-war, your most Illustrious Lordship received bad news. For that, acting as a faithful servant, I immediately went to the Palace to manifest to you the grief I bear for the death of Senhor Dom Vasco da Gama, (whom God has taken to his eternal mansion): but, as often as I went, I never could gain admittance, since your most Illustrious Lordship, being secluded in your apartments, naturally did not receive.

Notwithstanding, I call to your Lordship's mind, that you have been happy and fortunate in attaining what you wished and hoped for, viz: men-of-war safely arrived, with persons from Portugal, in time for the enterprise after "gold."

As the enterprise is, rather your most Illustrious Lordship's idea than mine,. I have no need to remind you the 13th of September is the most proper time to begin the voyage to Malacca; nor is there any occasion to exaggerate this affair of discovery, as your most Illustrious Lordship knows it well, and is well informed of everything in regard to it, and therefore will do what is most necessary, because when you think it is time for the discovery of the gold, I shall then receive my commission. If I do not receive it, I may yet attain my purpose, by soliciting protection for the enterprise.

At any rate, I cannot fail to call to your most Illustrious Lordship's attention, that the attainment of the discovery of the gold depends also upon the knowledge of the winds that blow on the "Mar do Oro" (sea of Gold); because without knowledge and forethought, there would be danger of meeting there the roughest weather in the world.

It must also be known that in the said "Mar do Oro," are to be encountered winter storms, from March to July; therefore, if I get my commission in this Moncao (monsoon) of September, I could stay in Malacca all November, and sail in December, for Solor, whence I could start by January, for Tymor, Ende or Sabbo, and winter in any of those islands. I could there obtain better information about the gold, and by August or September, by the help of Almighty God, start for the discovery of the happy "Island of Gold."

If I get my commission in April I should have to stay in Malacca, during June, July, August, September and October, and sail in December for Solor. Therefore ordain what may be most useful to the service of God, of the King, and of your most

Illustrious Lordship, as I am only your servant and an instrument for the discovery of this gold, as my conscience is urging me to embark in the said discovery, because God will help me to succeed, I therefore ask clamorously of your most Illustrious Lordship to employ me to obtain such a boon from whom it ought to come. May Jesus Christ guard you in health for the protection of this East India and of your servants. (Signed).

EM'EL GODINHO DE EREDIA.

MARQUIS D' AVILA E DE BOLAMA.

Among the modern statesmen by whom Portugal is honored, the Marquis d'Avila, born at Fayal in the Azores, is worthy of special mention. As a scientific man and as a political personage, he has not ceased to play one of the most marked roles in the affairs of Portugal, for more than forty years; first, in the quality of deputy to the Cortes for twenty-six years, and afterwards as a Cabinet Minister and Counsellor of State. Endowed with a very varied instruction and indefatigable in work, the Marquis d'Avila knew how to multiply his activity, and to apply himself under several forms, to the profit of the nation. We see him assisting in the counsels of the kingdom during the most difficult epochs, and at the same time taking part in the labors of the Academy of Science, watching in' the national industry, and assuming the superior direction of the credit establishments, instituted for the development of agriculture. A delegate to the Congress of statistics in Brussels, 1853, Paris, 1855, and Berlin 1863, and at the Congress for the unification of coins in 1867, as well as Royal Commissioner for the International Exhibition in Paris, he has acquired for himself a distinguished rank among his colleagues. In 1865, he represented Portugal in Madrid, as Minister Plenipotentiary, and held the same charge in Paris in 1868. In 1870, he was the President of the Cabinet and Minister for Foreign Affairs. To-day he performs the high functions of Counsellor of State and President of the Chamber of Peers. Whether as savant, orator, cabinet minister or diplomatist, his character has always been brilliant

and honorable; the laws of which he took the initiative in the
Chambers, his part also in the labors of different Congress, as
well as the reports he has written concerning his missions in
foreign countries, sustains his reputation at home and abroad.

INDEX.

EXPLANATORY AND ERRATA.

Milreis = 1,000 reis = $1,084.   Conto of reis = 1.000,000 reis = $1,084.

<table>
<tr><td colspan="3" align="center">PAGE.</td><td colspan="3" align="center">PAGE.</td></tr>
<tr><td>ennobled instead of enobled. ......7</td><td></td><td></td><td>Mm. de Bomfim</td><td>Mon. de Bonfine 45</td><td></td></tr>
<tr><td>Peninsula</td><td>"</td><td>Peninsular....10</td><td>Saldanha</td><td>"</td><td>Saldhana......47</td></tr>
<tr><td>Devastated</td><td>"</td><td>Devasted......11</td><td colspan="3">Jervis d'Athoguia instead of Jerois</td></tr>
<tr><td>Zezere</td><td>"</td><td>Bezere ......11</td><td></td><td>d'Althoneguia...............48</td><td></td></tr>
<tr><td colspan="3">It must be admitted that there have</td><td>Seabra instead of Sleabra.......48</td><td></td><td></td></tr>
<tr><td colspan="3">have been a few epedemics on the</td><td>Magalhaes</td><td>"</td><td>Magulhaes.....48</td></tr>
<tr><td>Continent...................12</td><td></td><td></td><td>Oratorical</td><td>"</td><td>Oratorica......49</td></tr>
<tr><td colspan="3">Leagues instead of Leaguse......13</td><td>Development</td><td>Developement..53</td><td></td></tr>
<tr><td>Longitude</td><td>"</td><td>Longtitude .. 13</td><td>Lope</td><td>"</td><td>Cope..........56</td></tr>
<tr><td>Angra</td><td>"</td><td>Augra........15</td><td>Vicente</td><td>"</td><td>bicente... ....58</td></tr>
<tr><td>Visigoths</td><td>"</td><td>Vieigoths......17</td><td>Silva</td><td>"</td><td>Silra..........58</td></tr>
<tr><td>Portuguese</td><td>"</td><td>Portuguse.....21</td><td>Ciumes</td><td>"</td><td>Cnimes........58</td></tr>
<tr><td>Apparant</td><td>"</td><td>Appearant.....25</td><td>valiant</td><td>"</td><td>radi-nt......70</td></tr>
<tr><td>Loanda</td><td>"</td><td>hoando........32</td><td>Hierarchy</td><td>"</td><td>Heirarchy.....81</td></tr>
<tr><td>Vassalage</td><td>"</td><td>Vasalage......33</td><td>Leonce</td><td>"</td><td>Leince........87</td></tr>
<tr><td>Incalculable</td><td>"</td><td>Incalcuable....35</td><td>Lupines</td><td>"</td><td>Luwines........87</td></tr>
<tr><td>Beresford</td><td>'</td><td>Bresford......39</td><td>Aveiro</td><td>"</td><td>Aviro.........95</td></tr>
<tr><td>Absolutism</td><td>"</td><td>Absoluteism....41</td><td>Sacavem</td><td>"</td><td>Sacavene.....96</td></tr>
<tr><td>Villaflor</td><td>"</td><td>Villaflon......41</td><td>Contos</td><td>"</td><td>Centos........97</td></tr>
<tr><td>Tagus</td><td>"</td><td>Sagus..... ..42</td><td colspan="3">The customs were 8,677 contos in</td></tr>
<tr><td>Capital</td><td>"</td><td>Capitol........43</td><td colspan="3">1860, or 20,200,000 francs</td></tr>
<tr><td>Terceira</td><td>"</td><td>Tercira........43</td><td>Culminating</td><td>"</td><td>Culminary....100</td></tr>
<tr><td colspan="3">Leuchtenberg   Luchtehnberg.. 43</td><td>Benguela</td><td>"</td><td>Benguael.....105</td></tr>
<tr><td>Granja</td><td>"</td><td>Graufa........44</td><td>Delgado</td><td>'</td><td>Delgudo......109</td></tr>
<tr><td>Hugon</td><td>"</td><td>Hugore........45</td><td>Timor</td><td>"</td><td>Fimor.......111</td></tr>
<tr><td>Terceira</td><td>"</td><td>Tericia ...... 45</td><td>Indigenous</td><td>"</td><td>Indigruous....112</td></tr>
<tr><td colspan="3">Carvalho instead of Carralho......44</td><td>Percentage</td><td>"</td><td>Precentage....128</td></tr>
</table>